NATIONALISM IN EUROPE, 1890–1940

Studies in European History

Series Editors: Richard Overy
John Breuilly
Peter Wilson

Nationalism in Europe, 1890–1940

Oliver Zimmer

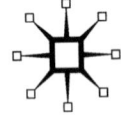
First published 2003 by
PALGRAVE MACMILLAN
Houndmills, Basingstoke, Hampshire RG21 6XS and
175 Fifth Avenue, New York, N.Y. 10010
Companies and representatives throughout the world

PALGRAVE MACMILLAN is the global academic imprint of
the Palgrave Macmillan division of St. Martin's Press, LLC and of
Palgrave Macmillan Ltd. Macmillan® is a registered trademark in the
United States, United Kingdom and other countries. Palgrave is a
registered trademark in the European Union and other countries.

ISBN 0–333–94720–7 paperback

This book is printed on paper suitable for recycling and made from
fully managed and sustained forest sources.

A catalogue record for this book is available from the British Library.

Library of Congress Cataloging-in-Publication Data

Zimmer, Oliver, 1964–
    Nationalism in Europe, 1890–1940 / Oliver Zimmer.
      p. cm. — (Studies in European history)
    Includes bibliographical references and index.
    ISBN 0–333–94720–7 (pbk.)
      1. Nationalism—Europe—History—19th century. 2. Nationalism—
Europe—History—20th century. 3. Self-determination, National. 4.
Fascism—Europe—History—20th century. 5. Europe—Ethnic relations.
I. Title. II. Studies in European history (Basingstoke, England)
D375.Z56 2003
320.54'094'09041—dc21
                                                                        2003049809

10   9   8   7   6   5   4   3   2   1
12   11   10   09   08   07   06   05   04   03

Typeset by Cambrian Typesetters, Frimley, Surrey
Printed in China

To my parents

Contents

vii

Editors' Preface

The main purpose of this new series of studies is to make available to teacher and student alike developments in a field of history that has become increasingly specialised with the sheer volume of new research and literature now produced. These studies are designed to present the 'state of the debate' on important themes and episodes in European history since the sixteenth century, presented in a clear and critical way by someone who is closely concerned with the debate in question.

The studies are not intended to be read as extended bibliographical essays, though each will contain a detailed guide to further reading which will lead students and the general reader quickly to key publications. Each book carries its own interpretation and conclusions, while locating the discussion firmly in the centre of the current issues as historians see them. It is intended that the series will introduce students to historical approaches which are in some cases very new and which, in the normal course of things, would take many years to filter down into the textbooks and school histories. We hope it will demonstrate some of the excitement historians, like scientists, feel as they work away in the vanguard of their subject. The series has an important contribution to make in publicising what it is that historians are doing and in making history more open and accessible. It is vital for history to communicate if it is to survive.

Acknowledgements

I am greatly indebted to the following colleagues for agreeing to read all or parts of the manuscript for this book: David Barry, John Breuilly, Sarah Davies, Jo Fox, Eric Kaufmann, Raymond Pearson, Kay Schiller and David Sweet. John Breuilly was extremely generous with advice and support from the moment I submitted the synopsis for this book. The responsibility for any errors and shortcomings it may still contain remains, of course, my own. Raymond Pearson gave me his kind permission to reproduce some of the statistical material from his *National Minorities in Eastern Europe, 1848–1945* (published in 1983) in the Appendix of this book. The students at Durham who attended my course on 'Nationalism in Europe in the Long Nineteenth Century: Debates and Developments' have enriched my thinking on the subject through numerous fruitful discussions.

MAP 1: The European empires in 1870

French Empire (legend pattern)
Germany (legend pattern)
Habsburg Empire (legend pattern)
Ottoman Empire (legend pattern)
Russian Empire (legend pattern)

NORWAY AND SWEDEN

FINLAND

St Petersburg

Baltic Sea

Moscow

North Sea

Riga

RUSSIAN EMPIRE

DENMARK

Königsberg

Heligoland (British)

EAST PRUSSIA

NETHERLANDS

Berlin

BELGIUM

GERMANY
Empire proclaimed in January 1871

Warsaw

Kiev

POLAND

Paris

SILESIA

LUXEMBOURG

Prague

Cracow

GALICIA

FRENCH EMPIRE

BAVARIA

HABSBURG

Munich

Vienna

BESSARABIA

Odessa

SWITZERLAND

Budapest

EMPIRE

Trieste

ROMANIA
Autonomous

Black Sea

Belgrade

Bucharest

SERBIA
Autonomous

BOSNIA

ITALY

Adriatic Sea

BULGARIA
Autonomous

Sofia

CORSICA (French)

Rome

MONTENEGRO

Constantinople

SARDINIA (Italian)

OTTOMAN EMPIRE

Corfu (Greek)

GREECE

0   100   200   300 miles

MAP 1: The European empires in 1870

xi

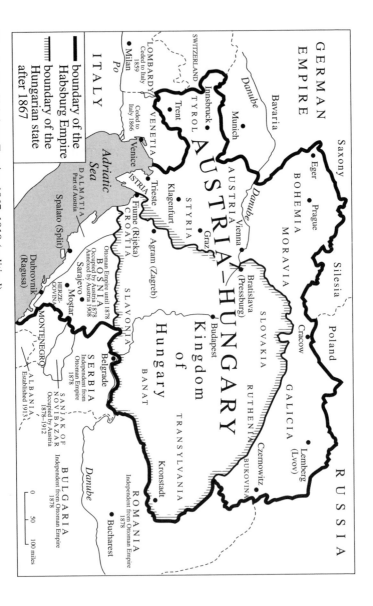

Map 2: The Habsburg Empire, 1867–1918 (political)

MAP 3: Europe after the peace settlements of 1919

xiii

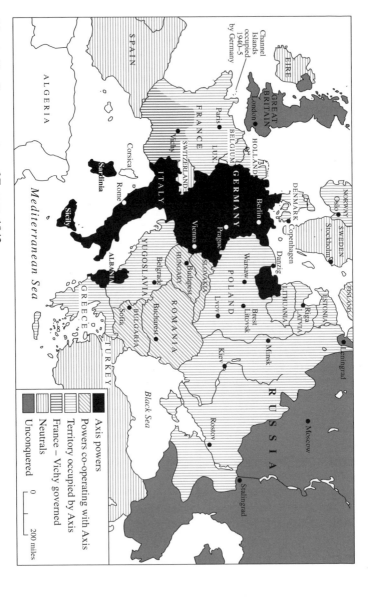

MAP 4: The German mastery of Europe, 1942

Introduction

'Nations are not something eternal. They began, so they will come to an end. A European confederation will probably replace them. But such is not the law of the age in which we live' [Renan in 19: p. 59]. So wrote the French historian Ernest Renan in his celebrated article *Qu'est-ce qu'une nation?* (1882), one of the richest and most original essays on the subject of national identity to appear in the nineteenth century.

The twentieth century would confirm Renan's double prediction. Nations and nationalism would indeed continue to play a key role in the history of Europe. At the same time, a European Community would take shape after the Second Word War. What Renan could not foresee was that this attempt at supranational integration would arise as a deliberate response to the most destructive events Europe had witnessed in its long and by no means peaceful history. Nor could he have predicted, from his nineteenth-century vantage point, that excessive forms of nationalism would play such a prominent part in this destruction. While nationalism had become a politically significant issue well before the late nineteenth century, it was between 1890 and 1940 – a period that witnessed the fall of several empires and the creation of numerous new states in central and eastern Europe, the rise of fascism, and the outbreak of the Second World War – that it revealed its full destructive potential.

The maps presented at the beginning of this book convey a sense of the geopolitical explosions that Europe witnessed during this period. The first two maps show a Europe in which large multi-ethnic empires covered most of the land surface of central and eastern Europe. The third map shows a Europe not of empires but of national states, many of which were created through the peace settlements that followed the First World War. Finally, the fourth map depicts Europe after Nazi Germany had embarked on its military conquest, resulting in the eradication, by 1940, of the states of Austria, Czechoslovakia, Poland, the Netherlands, Belgium and Luxembourg, with France being divided

1

into an occupied north and a south under the control of a collaborative regime.

Yet it would be misleading to reduce the history of nationalism in the period under consideration to a prelude to the Second World War and the horrors it produced. What part nationalism and its supporters played in the formation of fascism, the unleashing of large-scale military conflict, and in the systematic discrimination against, and persecution and murder of, ethnic minorities – these are questions that need analysing. They should not be regarded as foregone conclusions. As George Mosse argued in one of his last essays, condemning nationalism without distinction, or 'identifying it automatically with racism', deprives us of the possibility of understanding 'the most powerful ideology of modern times' [13: p. 168]. The 'mania for making judgements', to use a phrase by the great French historian Marc Bloch, who in 1944 became a victim of the Nazi conquest of Europe, should be resisted even when dealing with a subject as controversial as nationalism [11: p. 26].

One strategy for escaping the teleological fallacy that so often besets conventional textbooks on the subject is to adopt a more thematic and analytically focused approach. Thus although this book concentrates on a particular period in the history of nationalism, it does not provide a chronological narrative [for such narratives, see 9; 15; 18]. Instead, the text is organised around specific themes, many of which have been hotly debated by experts in recent years. The result is an account that is more explicitly focused on conceptual issues than most historical textbooks on the subject, yet also more historical (and more specifically historiographical) than most of the existing theoretical overviews [for introductions to the theoretical debate, see 16; 17; Breuilly in 19; Breuilly in 10; 12].

The book is divided into five chapters. Chapter 1 takes up the theoretical controversy over the modernity of nations and nationalism, outlining some of the most prominent interpretations and exploring the possible links between national consciousness and modern nationalism. Chapter 2 describes and explains the development of nationalism into a mass phenomenon after 1870, focusing on the role of the nationalising state, imperialism and inter-state competition, the significance of national rituals and festivals, and the impact of nationalism on regional identities. Chapter 3 highlights the ways in which nationalist arguments and policies influenced the treatment of minorities both before and particularly after the First World War. Chapter 4 explores the relationship between nationalism and fascism, stressing the crucial part of revisionist forms of nationalism for fascist mobilisation in the context of

2

geopolitical turmoil and consequent status deprivation among formerly dominant groups. Finally, Chapter 5 looks at the perception of nationalism by liberals and socialists.

The five chapters differ slightly in terms of analytical emphasis. Chapter 1 has a strong conceptual orientation, while Chapters 3 and 5 are mainly concerned with specific historical developments. Chapters 2 and 4 combine, in equal measure, conceptual, historiographical and historical aspects.

My aim has not been to offer a comprehensive account but rather to highlight particular phenomena and problems by using specific examples. The emphasis of Chapter 2 is on western and central Europe, especially France and Germany, and chronologically the decades prior to the First World War are in the foreground. In Chapters 3–5 the focus shifts further eastwards, with Germany, Poland, Romania, Czechoslovakia and Hungary providing the main examples. This methodological procedure – that is, examining a number of selected cases in somewhat greater detail and with the occasional reference to contemporary statements – struck me as more satisfying than a more impressionistic approach in which a dozen cases are used for illustrative purposes.

1   Nations and Nationalism: Ancient or Modern?

Why start this book with a chapter on theories and concepts? The question is worth posing. While genuine progress in the study of nationalism will always result from innovative historical research, it is nevertheless important that historians continue to engage with the theoretical frameworks available. Not because these models provide answers to key questions. Most historians will always remain highly sceptical of general theories of nationalism, and a spate of innovative recent case studies has increased rather than removed existing doubts regarding their general applicability. As this and subsequent chapters will show, there is now a movement away from the grand theories of nationalism (to which all students in the field remain indebted) and towards more specific conceptual debates and controversies. Even so, as ideal types, concepts and theories offer a foil of comparison and contrast that can help facilitate communication between scholars working in different chronological and geographical areas.

The conceptual debate

Is nationalism an inevitable by-product of the modern age, or do its origins stretch further back in time? And what about the temporal origins of the communities we commonly refer to as 'nations'?

Carl J. Friedrich addressed these questions more than 30 years ago in an influential reader on nation-building edited by Karl W. Deutsch and William J. Foltz. His answer was that we must distinguish between, on the one hand, the 'old' nations of the West (especially France and England), which developed more or less continuously out of medieval kingdoms into modern nations, and, on the other, the nations that sprang

4

up in the post-colonial world, which were deliberate constructions [Friedrich in 31: p. 1966]. The leading theorist of modern nationalism, Ernest Gellner, in a public address delivered shortly before his death in November 1995, asked about the origins of both nations and nationalism (which in his view arose together): 'Do nations have navels?' His answer: 'Some nations have it and some don't and in any case it's inessential' [35: 366–7].

Here we have a number of the most contested issues surrounding the history of nations and of nationalism: whether we can speak of pre-modern nations; whether pre-modern forms of national consciousness can be linked, in any politically significant way, to the rise of nationalism and of modern national identities; and finally, whether – or rather, to what extent – such identities can be 'invented', 'constructed' or 'imagined'. What seems least contentious at present concerns nationalism's temporal origins. That nationalism is a genuinely modern phenomenon that made its first appearance in Europe shortly before or after 1800 has almost assumed the status of a scholarly consensus. The majority of the leading scholars of nationalism – including Gellner, Hobsbawm, Anderson, Breuilly and Smith – have all linked the emergence of nationalism to specifically modern developments.

But if there is widespread agreement about the temporal origins of nationalism, there is far less agreement regarding its actual essence and, closely related, how it is best explained. Is nationalism primarily an ideology or political religion, a political movement seeking state power, a cultural formation allowing industrial societies to function, a modern cognitive framework, a movement of cultural and historical revival, or a combination of all these factors? A second, closely related, controversy concerns the causal links between pre-modern national consciousness (some authors have used the concepts of ethnicity, 'nation', or 'patriotism') and modern nationalism. Before we can consider in some detail the question concerning the relationship between pre-modern and modern nationhood, we have to outline these rival explanations of nationalism as a modern historical phenomenon.

The modernist consensus

Nationalism as ideology

To start with ideology is to start with the factor most closely associated with common-sense understandings of nationalism. In popular history books and in the printed and electronic media alike, nationalism is for the most part treated as an ideology or political religion. Early exponents of this viewpoint include Carlton Hayes and Hans Kohn. A more recent, and particularly influential, statement taking this line is Elie Kedorie's book *Nationalism* (first published in 1960). Kedourie defines nationalism as a 'doctrine invented in Europe at the beginning of the nineteenth century . . . Briefly, the doctrine holds that humanity is naturally divided into nations, that nations are known by certain characteristics which can be ascertained, and that the only legitimate type of government is national self-determination.' This doctrine, Kedourie asserts, provided a principle to legitimate a specific type of government – 'national self-government' – and international organisation – a 'society of states' [43: p. 1]. According to Kedourie, it quickly assumed the status of a self-evident framework that shaped the institutional fabric of modern society.

What distinguishes Kedourie's account from most of the others we shall discuss in this chapter is not that he defines nationalism as an ideology – this is rather common, as we shall see when we discuss the theories of Gellner, Hobsbawm, Breuilly and Smith. What sets it apart is that it treats nationalism as an ideology that needs to be explained by reference to ideological factors. Rejecting the materialist logic informing the theories of Gellner and others, in which nationalist ideology appears as a mere reflection of structural change, Kedourie sees nationalism as the outcome of a complex interaction between politics and ideas. In this dynamic process, the French Revolution played a central role. Specifically, in the Declaration of the Rights of Men, the nation was declared the sovereign of state power and the sole source of legitimate authority. From these revolutionary principles grew, in Kedourie's words, 'an eager expectation of change, a prejudice in its favour, and a belief that the state stagnated unless it was constantly innovating'. These expectations and demands for constant innovation found expression in a new kind of politics – what Kedourie calls 'ideological politics' [43: p. 5].

Yet for Kedourie, it was not the French Revolution that produced nationalism as a political doctrine. Rather, nationalism resulted from the fusion of three momentous philosophical ideas, which in the early nineteenth century began to acquire political significance. Because the thinkers who fostered these ideas were German, Kedourie argues that nationalism was a German intellectual invention. The three ideas are Immanuel Kant's (1724–1804) idea of individual self-determination, Johann Gottlieb Fichte's (1762–1814) idea that the social whole is more important than its individual parts, and Johann Gottfried Herder's (1744–1803) emphasis on the value of ethnolinguistic diversity.

According to Kant, people cannot find true freedom, morality and virtue in the external world but only in the laws of morality they find in themselves. Thus the struggle for individual self-determination becomes the supreme political good [43: p. 19]. One of Kant's most influential disciples, Johann Gottlieb Fichte, began to conceive of self-determination in collectivistic rather than individualistic terms. To be more precise, he regarded the universe as an organic whole, 'no part of which can exist without the existence of all the rest'. Consequently – and this, according to Kedourie, is Fichte's contribution to the doctrine of nationalism – the freedom of the individual lies in identifying himself with the social whole [43: pp. 29–30]. The third idea received its most mature philosophical expression in the work of Herder. Challenging the notion that progress meant regularity, uniformity, maturity and rationality, which lay at the heart of the French Enlightenment, Herder emphasised the intrinsic value of cultural diversity. This cultural diversity was embodied in the various ethnic groups and nations, who found their most authentic expression in their communal languages. Breuilly sums up Herder's view of language as the key to national authenticity thus: 'If language is thought, and can be learnt only in a community, it follows that each community has its own mode of thought' [28: p. 57].

Thus emerged, in Kedourie's view, a conception of nationhood radically different from that promoted by the French revolutionaries. The conception of nationality entertained by the French revolutionaries 'meant a number of individuals who have opted in favour of a certain kind of government'. By contrast, the German conception saw in the nation an expression of 'the natural division' of humanity that 'its citizens must, as a duty, preserve pure and inviolable' [43: p. 51]. Combining the notion of cultural diversity with his own ideas of collective self-determination, Fichte wrote on the state of Germany in 1807, still under the influence of Prussia's defeat at Jena and Auerstaedt in the previous year:

> The separation of Prussians from the rest of the Germans is purely artificial . . . The separation of the Germans from the other European nations is based on nature. Through a common language and through common national characteristics which unite the Germans, they are separable from the others. [43: p. 63]

Nationalism as a historicist response to the crisis of Enlightenment absolutism

Another, today rather neglected, type of explanation locates the origins of nationalism in a crisis of meaning and orientation in the late eighteenth century. Rather than concentrating on philosophical ideas and their interaction, its exponents have pointed to the role of historicism as a movement of cultural regeneration directed against the eighteenth-century state and its rational administration. Although this paradigm still operates within the assumption that nationalism is modern, it traces its beginnings in the decades preceding the French Revolution. Its proponents also insist that nationalism is not just about political self-government but often involves a preoccupation with historical origins and cultural authenticity. This type of explanation has found expression in a number of essays by Isaiah Berlin, while a more sociological version can be found in some of the earlier works of Anthony D. Smith.

According to Berlin, ethnohistoricism was essentially a movement of the counter-Enlightenment. Whereas the Enlightenment, at least in its French version, assumed that human societies were determined by certain timeless and universal laws that science would eventually reveal, thinkers such as Giovanni Battista Vico (1668–1744), Johann Gottfried Herder, Jean-Jacques Rousseau (1712–78) and Edmund Burke (1729–97) began to challenge these presumptions [26: 1–24]. Truth, they insisted, was not timeless but embedded in specific historical traditions and unique culture communities which expressed themselves in a great variety of languages, rituals, monuments and mythologies. These cultural manifestations of human activity were seen as a key to the consciousness and character of a particular community [see 25; 23].

While sharing Berlin's basic tenets, Anthony Smith has attributed the historicist revolution of the late eighteenth century much more specifically to the activities of secular intellectuals and their complex and often anomie-ridden position within the system of Enlightened absolutism. An evolutionary historicism, Smith argues, 'became the cultural framework and basis of nationalism', first in Europe and, if much later, outside the Old Continent [48: p. 88; for neo-classical and Romantic versions of historicism, see 47]. Historicist intellectuals endeavoured to reconstruct the history and life of authentic culture communities because they regarded this as the key to their character and their true *Wesen*. In language and literature, in music and the visual arts, this historicist

8

agenda became visible. It also served as the main inspiration for the new academic disciplines of archaeology and history.

From this perspective, the rise of historicist nationalism appears as a response by the rapidly growing new strata of intellectuals and educators to the normative contradictions resulting from the spread of Enlightenment values within a society whose legitimacy still rested on traditional principles of social hierarchy and moral authority. Many of these intellectuals and educators were serving, at some point and in some capacity or other, absolutist-style governments. As champions of an enlightened style of government they attempted to infuse the traditional order with enlightened ideals of progress, rationality and achievement. By taking measures designed to fight administrative and economic inefficiency, regional particularism, aristocratic privilege and exclusive forms of representation, enlightened rulers introduced quasi-modern notions of equality and justice into the political arena. There was, in Eric Hobsbawm's words, 'virtually no prince from Madrid to St Petersburg and from Naples to Stockholm who did not, at one time or another in the quarter-century preceding the French Revolution, subscribe to such a programme' [39: p. 37]. Yet because these programmes remained ultimately committed to the preservation of an order of estates, they caused resentment among the educated new strata whose members, in terms of their influence and external recognition, still remained in a marginal position. It is here that ethnohistoricism, and ultimately nationalism, was sometimes adopted as a language of opposition to the existing order [48: chs. 5 and 6; on enlightened forms of absolutist rule, see also 21: pp. 15–42 and 46: introduction; for specific case studies of eighteenth-century nationalism which discuss the role of historicism, see 24: chs. 4 and 5; 55: ch. 2].

Nationalism as political movement

The most influential account treating nationalism as a political phenomenon can be found in John Breuilly's *Nationalism and the State*. Breuilly reserves the term 'nationalism' for 'political movements seeking or exercising state power and justifying such action with nationalist arguments'. The political doctrine of nationalism, Breuilly writes, is built on 'three basic assertions': that there 'exists a nation with an explicit and peculiar character'; that the 'interests and values of this nation take priority over all other interests and values'; and that the 'nation must be as independent as possible' [28: p. 2]. Breuilly's central categories are political movement and the modern state. It is the dynamic interaction between these two factors that provides the engine of modern nationalism.

However, by prioritising the state and political movements, Breuilly does not wish to deny the central role of the doctrinal dimension of nationalism. In a way similar to Smith, Breuilly explains the rise of nationalist argument as a result of the crisis of the modern bureaucratic state. Nationalists, in his view, try to bridge the widening gulf between increasingly powerful state and civil society. This split occurred in the modern era, particularly with the rise of a free-market economy, provoking a number of questions that began to preoccupy the minds of intellectuals from the late eighteenth century onwards. What is society? Is it just an aggregation of individuals? What is its status? Can it be changed? Nationalism provides an answer to these questions and problems – Breuilly calls it a 'pseudo-solution' – by focusing on history and culture. From this historicist point of view, what is emphasised is the historical and cultural uniqueness of a great variety of communities that make up human society as a whole. In modern nationalist ideology, the 'nation' – the cultural and historical community – and state – the political and institutional manifestation of that community – become fused [28: pp. 69–70].

Yet although Breuilly concedes the fundamental importance of nationalist intellectuals, he is critical of a pure intellectual history approach as developed by Kedourie and others. Rather than simply focusing on ideas and their continuous elaboration, Breuilly urges us to examine the causes for their political significance. It is only when nationalist ideas and ideologies are taken up and implemented by political movements that they come to shape historical reality in any significant way [Breuilly in 10: p. 148]. It is above all in the struggle over the modern state, Breuilly contends, that nationalist ideas acquire political significance by serving three important functions. The first is *interest co-ordination*. Nationalist ideas were used to 'promote the idea of common interests amongst a number of elites which otherwise have rather distinct interests in opposing the existing state'. The second is *mobilisation*. Here Breuilly refers to the 'use of nationalist ideas to generate support for the political movement from broad groups hitherto excluded from the political process'. Finally, nationalist arguments serve as a legitimisation for the goals of a political movement, be that goal the reform of the given order (the western European pattern of nationalism), the separation of a cultural community from an existing state (the

Habsburg and Ottoman scenario), or the unification of a number of territorial states into a single nation-state (the Italian and German pattern)
[Breuilly in 10: pp. 166–7].

Nationalism as the cultural glue of industrial societies

With the work of Ernest Gellner we enter a radically different territory.
Although he also defines nationalism as a 'political principle' and a
'theory of political legitimacy' that required that 'ethnic boundaries
should not cut across political ones', Gellner locates its causes in the
structural processes that enabled the transition from agrarian to industrial societies [33: p. 1]. Hence, if Kedourie sees the essence of nationalism in a fateful fusion of a set of ideas, Gellner regards it as a
by-product of the structural transformations that brought about modern
society. In contrast to the historically specific accounts of Kedourie,
Berlin, Smith and Breuilly, Gellner has developed a model that claims to
explain nationalism in general.

Put succinctly, Gellner maintains that nationalism arose in the modern
period because industrial societies, unlike pre-modern agrarian ones, need
homogenous, language-based high cultures in order to work efficiently. It
is the modern state and its educated personnel who perform this task by
mobilising campaigns of assimilation mainly through public education.
Under the conditions of modern, industrialised societies with their
demands on the mobility of labour, these institutionalised high cultures take
the role that in pre-modern societies was fulfilled by ascribed social roles
and clearly defined social relations. As Gellner explains the pivotal role of
cultural communication for modern societies: 'The capacity to move
between diverse jobs, and incidentally to communicate and cooperate with
numerous individuals in other social positions, requires that members of
such a society be able to communicate in speech and writing, in a formal,
precise, context-free manner – in other words they must be educated, literate and capable of orderly, standardised presentation of messages' [34: p.
15]. Thus for Gellner, it is not free-floating ideas or ideologies that represent the essence of nationalism. His anti-idealism comes out most clearly
in his critique of the view which holds that nationalism 'might not have
happened, if only those damned busy-body interfering European thinkers
... had not concocted it and fatefully injected it into the bloodstream of
otherwise viable political communities' [33: p. 56].

At the same time, this modern, language-based culture becomes visible and a source of pride and focus of collective identification. It is this

11

identification with linguistic high cultures – rather than ideas about national self-determination entertained by a few German philosophers or the folk culture glorified by Romantic nationalists – that in Gellner's view constitutes and sustains both nations and nationalism. This identification is achieved through cultural standardisation and homogenisation. Citizens are taught a single language and forget the dialects that were the outward manifestation of the cultural diversity that characterised pre-modern societies. Gellner does not deny the emotive pull of nationalism, but he warns against confusing nationalism's appeal with its causes. The fact that nationalism appealed perhaps more to people's hearts and souls than to their minds, he repeatedly insists, should not lure us into adopting a psychological explanation. Such explanations, which tend to emphasise peoples' need to belong, he considers quite misleading. As he puts it in *Thought and Change*:

> The self-image of nationalism involves the stress on folk, folklore, popular culture, etc. In fact, nationalism becomes important precisely when these things become artificial. Genuine peasants or tribesmen, however proficient at folk-dancing, do not generally make good nationalists. It is only when a privileged cousin of the same lineage, and later their own sons, and finally even their own daughters, all go to school, that the peasant or tribesman acquires a vested interest in the language that was employed in the school in which that cousin, son or daughter were educated. [32: p. 161]

Obviously Gellner's model can be applied with some success to western and central Europe, but what about the rise of nationalism in those societies that remained little touched by industrialisation for some time to come? What about eastern Europe in the nineteenth century, or Africa and Asia in the twentieth? Gellner is of course aware that industrialisation proceeded unevenly, and that much of the world remained predominantly agricultural even after nationalism had become a force in some parts of Europe around the turn of the eighteenth century. This was the case, for example, in the Habsburg and Ottoman empires, where nationalism became visible among the members of economically backward nationalities. This was, Gellner argues, because of a clash between dominant and subordinate cultures. It was only with the coincidence of administrative centralisation by enlightened rulers on the one hand, and the increasing cultural awareness resulting from economic modernisation on the other, that this exclusion became politicised and existing grievances were expressed in nationalist terms. This is how Gellner explains the nationalism of the Czechs, Serbs, Croatians, Greeks, etc.,

12

which rapidly gained momentum in the second half of the nineteenth century [32: p. 158].

Nationalism as cultural construction

The most influential works on nationalism to have stressed the aspect of construction are those of Eric Hobsbawm and Benedict Anderson. Yet although both have seen in a process of cultural construction an essential feature of modern nationalism, there are marked differences in the way in which they conceive of construction and of the functions it fulfils in the formation and reproduction of modern national identities.

In his *Nations and Nationalism since 1780* (1990), and particularly in the influential collection entitled *The Invention of Tradition* (1983), Hobsbawm fashioned a concept of cultural construction that emphasises the role of official cultural politics and other manifestations of nationalist ritual that became such a conspicuous feature in nineteenth-century Europe. Like Breuilly, Hobsbawm regards nationalism primarily as a political phenomenon. But whereas the former sees nationalism as a response to a crisis of meaning and attributes its political significance to its ability to mobilise, co-ordinate and legitimate collective action in struggles over state power, Hobsbawm's model is much more elite-centred. Thus for him, nationalism offers a device for political legitimation. It was particularly in the second half of the nineteenth century, Hobsbawm argues, that the question of political legitimacy acquired a new urgency and nationalism became a mass phenomenon. The rapid social change that was unleashed during the second wave of industrialisation, in the late nineteenth century, went hand in hand with increased alienation and insecurity; invented traditions responded to this challenge by historicising the present, conveying a sense of invariance and stability in a world of constant change [38: introduction].

But there were more specific reasons why nationalism gained currency in the late nineteenth century. Above all, this was the beginning of the era of 'electoral democracy', when the masses were 'invited into history'. This (however gradual and uneven) expansion of political participation rights created a fundamental challenge to the authority and legitimacy of traditional power elites. In this situation, nationalism offered a promising ideological device to shore up a potentially endangered power base, an ideological tool to secure state authority in an era of mass democracy. It was thus anything but an accident, Hobsbawm argues, that elites developed an interest in the promotion and dissemination of national values through schooling and military education, as well as through the invention of public national ceremonies, rituals and symbols. Conceding that the 'most successful examples of manipulation are those which exploit practices which clearly meet a felt ... need among particular bodies of people' [38: p. 107], he writes in his introduction to the collection:

> [Invented traditions] ... are highly relevant to that comparatively recent historical innovation, the 'nation', with its associated phenomena: nationalism, the nation-state, national symbols, histories and the rest. All these rest on exercises in social engineering which are often deliberate and always innovative, if only because historical novelty implies innovation. [38: p. 13]

Benedict Anderson's concept of the nation as an 'imagined political community' shares with Hobsbawm an emphasis on cultural construction. But Anderson views nationalism essentially as a new cognitive formation rather than an ideological device to legitimate authority. Nations are imagined communities, he tells us, because all communities larger than villages with face-to-face contact are. The nation's members will never know most of their fellow members, 'yet in the minds of each lives the image of their communion' [20: p. 6]. But nationalism is a particular form of communal imagining: the nation is imagined as a limited, exclusive and sovereign community. To this definition Anderson adds the observation that nations exert a powerful emotive spell; that their members perceive them as communities worthy of the ultimate sacrifice of one's life. This is the case, Anderson tells us, because nationalism represents a response to the crisis of meaning and orientation that results from the decline of religious and dynastic authority since the sixteenth century. Like religion, nationalism addresses the problem of the contingency of human life, and particularly the issues of death and of suffering. It does so, Anderson argues, by transforming 'fatality into continuity, contingency into meaning' [20: p. 12].

But there were also positive conditions why this particular style of imagining – nationalism – came about. Of particular importance was the rise of 'print-capitalism' in the wake of the Protestant Reformation, when the Bible began to appear in the vernacular languages. Luther's theses, for example, were printed in German and within 15 days had been seen in every part of the country. Protestantism made effective use of the expanding vernacular print market, while the Counter-Reformation tried to preserve Latin as the sacred language of

Christendom. Other means of vernacular-based mass communication followed in the eighteenth and nineteenth centuries, particularly the novel and the newspaper. The languages in which books and newspapers were printed laid the basis for the emergence of the new cognitive style which, in turn, enabled the emergence of national consciousness – first, because they created 'unified fields of exchange and communications below Latin and above the spoken vernaculars', and second, because they gave 'a new fixity to language'. Hence the gist of Anderson's argument is this: it was Gutenberg's invention of printing that made possible the idea of a secular, imagined linguistic community, but it was commodity capitalism that made a particular kind of such community, the nation, likely [20: p. 36].

Pre-modern nationalism?: the minority view

The predominance of the modernist viewpoint notwithstanding, however, there have been a few dissenting voices. Most recently, the English medievalist Adrian Hastings has launched a fundamental critique of the modernist theories of nationalism just discussed. In his much-noticed book *The Construction of Nationhood: Ethnicity, Religion and Nationalism,* Hastings argues that while the doctrine of national self-determination did not become significant until the nineteenth century, nationalism had 'existed as a powerful reality in some places long before that'. Thus according to Hastings, the pre-modern period knew both nations and nationalism. In England in particular, he contends, a 'nationalism of a sort was present in the fourteenth century in the long wars with France and still more in the sixteenth and seventeenth' [37: p. 5]. But even where nationalist sentiment developed later in the early modern period, pre-modern nations often took shape considerably earlier. The force that often transformed ethnic affiliations into the more self-conscious nations was vernacular literature, 'particularly a religious and legal literature'. As Hastings concludes: 'Oral languages are proper to ethnicities; widely written vernaculars to nations' [37: pp. 20–1].

What has remained somewhat controversial about Hastings's account, and may have weakened its potential impact, is his dating of nationalism back into the medieval period. Hastings did not arrive at this conclusion on the basis of new empirical evidence on medieval England. Rather, what allowed him to locate nationalism in the fourteenth century was his rather broad definition of nationalism. Thus for Hastings, nationalism is best understood as a highly self-conscious national identity combined with strong feelings of ethnocentrism, expressed in religiously underpinned antipathies towards other culture communities. [For a similarly broad understanding of nationalism, see 27: 15–25, 232–4, 279–83.] Such a broad definition seems to hinder rather than further our understanding of the complex genesis of nationalism.

In what is still the most extensive exploration of the problem of how nationalism might be defined, Anthony D. Smith has advocated a sharp separation of ethnocentrism and nationalism. While ethnocentrism represents a near-universal phenomenon that can be found in most ancient kingdoms, nationalism, Smith insists, is a thoroughly modern phenomenon [49: ch. 1]. More recently, John Breuilly has made the point that broad definitions of nationalism lead to the creation of an 'impossibly large subject'. He therefore suggests that nationalism, as a concept, should be restricted to those statements 'which make the idea of a peculiar nation explicit' and make it 'the foundation of all political claims' [28: p. 3]. It is particularly the second aspect – the use of nation as a politically significant rather than purely descriptive concept – that is absent in Hastings's definition.

A more persuasive critique of the modernist viewpoint has been advanced in an extensive recent article by Philip S. Gorski. Gorski's broader contention is that nations (i.e. extensive cultural communities displaying an explicit sense of self-awareness) and nationalism tend to arise together. But unlike modernists such as Gellner, he argues that in a few cases – particularly in England and the Netherlands – this dual formation took place in the early modern period. Focusing primarily on the Dutch case, Gorski argues that there are 'clear examples of nationalism . . . in the early-modern period' [36: p. 1429]. Although he concedes that these pre-modern manifestations of nationalist sentiment may differ in some respects from those that emerged during and after the American and French revolutions – the latter display a much more secular rhetoric, while the former tend to be couched in religious idioms – he nevertheless argues that they are sufficiently similar to warrant inclusion under the label nationalism. What has prevented this, he argues, is that the modernist position 'rests on a distorted . . . picture of early modern political culture' [36: p. 1456].

Dutch nationalism, Gorski contends, arose in the sixteenth century in the context of the Dutch revolt against Spain (c.1555–1609). It was directed against the Habsburgs' policy of administrative penetration and was reinforced by the confessional conflict between Dutch Calvinism and Catholicism. In the course of this conflict, Dutch historians, pamphleteers, song-writers and ministers drew on 'symbols and stories of the Old Testament' to justify their resistance to Habsburg rule. Gorski uses the term 'holy or Hebraic nationalism' to denote the central place of the concept of the chosen people in this incipient and widely popular Dutch nationalism. Building on this ideological foundation, the seventeenth century saw the formation of a Batavian nationalism that emphasised political sovereignty, portraying it as 'a precondition of true nationhood'. Initially this second, republican, nationalism possessed less popular resonance than Hebraic nationalism. However, by the 1670s the two narratives – the Hebraic and the Batavian – had become closely intertwined, thus increasing the social scope of early modern Dutch nationalism [36: pp. 1436–50].

Given that by Gorski's own admission the republican discourse of the Dutch nation was limited in social scope, much hinges on the empirical validity of his argument that the two were fused productively towards the close of the seventeenth century. The concept of the chosen people and of the special covenant with God – which in Gorski's view also represents nationalism – had acquired wide application in Europe since the medieval period. It was also distinct in many ways from the kind of nationalism we associate with the French Revolution and other modern nationalist movements. Yet the strength of Gorski's argument lies in the fact that the Batavian narrative – with its emphasis on sovereignty and self-determination – does indeed contain central components of modern nationalist ideology. Based on the evidence he presents, one is tempted to conclude that a decidedly political brand of nationalism developed conspicuously early in the Dutch case, at least a century before it emerged in France and subsequently in other European countries. (Much less convincing is Gorski's proposition, made in the final section of his essay, to 'define nationalism as any set of discourses or practices that invoke "the nation" or equivalent categories' [see 36: p. 1461].)

One way of summarising the controversy over the modernity of nationalism might be to say that much hinges on the definitions applied. The modernist position possesses considerable heuristic advantages over that of its critics because its exponents work with a relatively narrow definition. If we begin to regard ethnocentrist sentiment and the descriptive use of the word 'nation' by a few medieval clerics as manifestations of nationalism, then few forms of collective self-assertion (whether they entail the semantics of 'nation' or not) would not qualify for inclusion. Nationalism would become a near-meaningless concept. Even the wide application of the notion of the chosen people in the medieval and early modern world should not be too readily associated with nationalism. True, many modern nationalist movements have made frequent use of these two narratives – that based on ethnocentrist stereotypes and that which draws on the notion of divine election – but these have usually been linked to demands for political self-government and communal regeneration in the name of 'the nation'. The late eighteenth-century patriots, with their preoccupation with 'national character', offer the first elaborate manifestation of this nationalist discourse that combined cultural and political concerns [see 54; 48: ch. 6; 24; 55: ch. 2].

This does not mean, however, that one should too readily discard the possibility of early modern (or for that matter, medieval) expressions of nationalism as a matter of principle. Gorski has pointed to one such possible exception, and future research might well reveal further examples of nationalism in the pre-modern world. Such possibilities cannot be ruled out on the basis of general theories or definitions that reduce nationalism to a purely political phenomenon or a function of modern industrial societies. But nor should they be simply assumed on the basis of vague definitions.

(Pre-modern) nations and (modern) nationalism: connections or continuities?

But there remains the more important question regarding the relationship between national awareness (or national sentiment) and nationalism. Here again the problem centres on the question of chronology and periodisation. If the view that there was nationalism before the late eighteenth century has remained highly controversial, there is relatively little disagreement that national consciousness has often predated the modern period. (Exceptions include the grand theorists of nationalism, Ernest Gellner and Benedict Anderson, who tend to equate nationalism and national awareness. By contrast, the historians Eric Hobsbawm and John Breuilly, as well as the historical sociologist Anthony Smith, explicitly distinguish between these two phenomena.) Thus the question arises about the relationship between national consciousness and nationalism. Does the existence of such antecedents facilitate, even accelerate, the genesis of modern nationalism? Or can modern nationalism do without them? To formulate the question by using Ernest Gellner's metaphor: Does modern nationalism need navels, or is it nationalism that creates nations (conceived as self-aware groups that refer to themselves in such terms) where they did not exist before?

Some scholars have insisted that any satisfactory explanation of nationalism requires us to take account of the pre-modern political and cultural formations referred to as 'nations'. Put simply, this view implies that there are fundamental links between pre-modern nations on the one hand, and modern nations and nationalism on the other, links that go beyond the descriptive. By ignoring these connections, so the assertion goes, the modernist theories of nationalism leave out a potentially important dimension.

Proto-national bonds

One (admittedly cautious) qualification of the modernist point of view along such lines has been advanced by Eric Hobsbawm, an author commonly closely identified with the modernist interpretation of nationalism. In his standard account of the subject, for example, he devotes a whole chapter to what he describes as 'proto-nationalism'. Ironically, this illuminating chapter on the possible political and cultural antecedents of modern nationalism has received much less attention than the rest of his book, which deals with the elaboration and dissemination of nationalism in the course of the long nineteenth century. Hobsbawm uses the term 'proto-nationalism' to refer to 'certain variants of feelings of collective belonging which already existed and which could operate, as it were, potentially on the macro-political scale which could fit in with modern states and nations'. Of special significance for modern nationalism, he writes, are 'political bonds and vocabularies of select groups more directly linked to states and institutions', because they 'are capable of eventual generalization, extension and popularization' [40: pp. 46, 47]. These quotations indicate that Hobsbawm conceives of the relationship between proto-national bonds and modern nationalism in terms of *connections* rather than continuities. Where proto-national bonds existed, he asserts in a key passage, they 'made the task of nationalism easier . . . insofar as existing symbols and sentiments of proto-national community could be mobilized behind a modern cause or a modern state' [40: p. 77].

At the same time, however, Hobsbawm cautions us against the assumption of an automatic continuity between pre-modern proto-nationalism and modern nationalism. Just as the setting up of a modern state is not sufficient in itself to create a nation, so the existence of proto-nationalism is not sufficient to create a modern nation-state. There is also a danger, he notes, of over-estimating the emotive appeal of a concept like 'nation' to ordinary people in the seventeenth and eighteenth centuries, let alone in earlier times. There are also problems of evidence facing historians trying to establish the exact social scope of pre-modern forms of national awareness and, even more, of national loyalty. Historians are thus 'running the risk', Hobsbawm warns, 'of giving the people marks in terms of a syllabus they have not studied and an examination they are not taking' [40: pp. 78–9].

Ethnosymbolic antecedents

The most systematic investigation into the links between pre-modern forms of national awareness (Smith uses the concept of ethnicity) and modern nationalism has been presented by Anthony D. Smith. Particularly in his book *The Ethnic Origins of Nations* (1986), as well as in several of his more recent contributions, Smith has argued that nationalism and modern national identities have stronger roots in pre-modern ethnicity than exponents of modernism such as Gellner, Hobsbawm and Breuilly are prepared to concede. In particular, he has emphasised the role of *ethnies* in the formation of nationalism and modern national identities. These he defines as 'named human populations with shared ancestry myths, histories and cultures, having an association with a specific territory, and a sense of solidarity' [50: p. 32]. Insisting that modern nations and nationalism need to be placed in the historical *longue durée,* Smith has pointed to the potential continuities (rather than merely connections) between pre-modern forms of ethnic and national awareness and modern nationalism.

Starting from these premises, Smith distinguishes between two routes to modern nation formation in the pre-modern period. The first he calls the 'imperial–dynastic route'. Here the impetus for nation formation derives from the power centre through bureaucratic incorporation of a relatively large subject population. This power centre is composed of an ethnic group of aristocratic, dynastic or clerical origin. Such upper-class ethnic groups often share a sense of common ethnicity and identity, embodied in myths of common descent and ethnic election. Yet given the exclusive character of these ethnic groups, the myths, cultural values and customs they create tend to lack social depth. Nevertheless, from the fourteenth and fifteenth centuries onwards, particularly in western Europe, such aristocratic ethnic communities began to institutionalise and territorialise their culture through the formation and expansion of bureaucratic states. In England, France, Spain and Sweden, an increasingly powerful state with its military, administrative, fiscal and judicial apparatus was 'able to regulate and disseminate the fund of values, symbols, myths, traditions and memories that formed the cultural heritage of the dominant ethnic core' [51: p. 55; on lateral ethnies, see 50: pp. 76–83].

The second path to modern nation formation Smith calls the 'communal demotic' route. Here the ethnic community is less exclusive, and its culture is shared by different classes rather than merely an exclusive elite. Quite often, such vertical or demotic ethnies were subject groups whose fate was totally or partially determined by a larger imperial power; and frequently, the former were religious frontier communities living in close proximity to more powerful groups who adhered to a different religion. Smith names the Orthodox Russians, the Gregorian Armenians, the Catholic Irish and Poles, as well as the Jews, as examples of such demotic ethnies. But while these vertical ethnies were held together by a rich and pervasive ethnocultural heritage, they lacked the power necessary for successful state formation. This not only explains why, quite often, the transformation of such ethnic communities into modern nation-states tended to take place comparatively late, i.e. in the late nineteenth or early twentieth century when nationalism had become a widely recognised discourse and institutionalised reality. It also accounts for the fact that members of the intelligentsia, usually of lower middle-class origin, tended to play a prominent part in the mobilisation of such ethnic groups. An example of this kind of nation formation is Ireland. The Gaelic revival of the 1890s in Ireland, and the national revival movements in eastern and south-eastern Europe of the late nineteenth century, provide cases in point [50: pp. 83–9; on Ireland, see 42].

According to Smith, what is significant in both these cases is that premodern ethnic groups often functioned as bearers of communal values and myth-symbol complexes. Through institutions such as the Christian church, kingdoms with their lateral *ethnies*, communal treaties, cults and customs, these myth-symbol complexes were often preserved and transmitted over centuries, thus facilitating the formation of nations in the modern period. Hence with his concept of ethnosymbolism Smith claims a potentially tighter link between pre-modern and modern nations than Hobsbawm does with his notion of proto-nationalism. Hobsbawm conceives of proto-national formations in terms of a toolkit from which modern political actors (and particularly nationalists) select certain elements depending on their situational needs. Smith, on the other hand, sees myth-symbol complexes and ethnohistories not just as resources, but as cultural structures that delimited the scope for the kind of elite-driven ideological activity which for Hobsbawm represents the hallmark of modern nationalism. As he puts his critique of the constructivist and instrumentalist view of national identity:

> Nationalists have a vital role to play in the construction of nations, not as culinary artists or social engineers, but as political archeologists rediscovering and reinterpreting the communal past in order to regenerate the community. Their task is indeed selective – they forget as well as remember the past – but to succeed in their task they must meet certain criteria. Their interpretations must be consonant not only with the ideological demands of nationalism, but also with the scientific evidence, popular resonance and patterning of particular ethno-histories. [52: p. 19]

Critics of ethnosymbolism

If Hobsbawm's concept of proto-nationalism has been relatively uncontroversial, Smith's insistence on the significance of ethnosymbolic antecedents for the formation of modern nations has provoked a number of criticisms. The reason is obvious. Although Hobsbawm points to possible connections between proto-nationalism and modern nationalist ideology, his argument does not alter his essentially modernist interpretation of nationalism. By contrast, Smith's ethnosymbolic approach represents an explicit critique of the modernist position. Although he does not claim direct or determinate links between pre-modern ethnies and modern nations – what distinguishes the latter from the former, he has repeatedly emphasised, is that modern nations possess legal, political and economic unity – he nevertheless regards existing ethnic myths and symbols as more than merely a resource from which actors can pick and choose.

The most explicit criticisms of Smith's point of view have come from John Breuilly and Ernest Gellner. Breuilly has expressed strong reservations about what he regards as Smith's implicit argument, namely, that 'the stronger and more persistent such [ethnic] identities, the more successful will be modern nationalism'. For Breuilly, this perspective assigns rather too much weight to pre-modern ethnic identity and its associated ethnosymbolism in the formation of modern nationalism. What distinguishes pre-modern forms of ethnic or national consciousness from modern ones, he argues, is that the former are 'non-institutional'. It is precisely the three elements that Smith admits are absent in pre-modern ethnies – legal, political and economic identity – that, according to Breuilly, were vital for the formation of modern national identities. As he argues: 'The problem with identity established outside institutions, especially those institutions which can bind together people across wide social and geographical spaces, is that it is necessarily fragmentary, discontinuous, and elusive' [Breuilly in 10: p. 151]. Breuilly concedes that there are cases where pre-modern ethnicity is embedded in important institutions such as the church or a dynasty. The problem here, however, is the lack of affinity, or fit, between these (in his view supranational) institutions and modern nationalism. Institutions such as the church or a dynasty, Breuilly claims, 'carry at their heart an alternative, ultimately conflicting sense of identity to that of the ethnic group' [Breuilly in 10: p. 151].

Ernest Gellner has expressed very similar reservations about Smith's insistence on the significance of pre-modern ethnicity for modern nationalism. Gellner's main point is that 'ethnicity' and 'ethnosymbolism' were not 'determinative': in other words, unlike the structural transformation brought about by industrialisation – the central thrust of Gellner's own theory of nationalism – they did not represent causal forces but were at best providing cultural resources for modern nationalist rhetoric. Where pre-modern nations and related forms of collective awareness were absent, nationalism would create nations where they did not exist, rendering the former irrelevant. As he puts his criticism in a characteristically trenchant passage:

> My main case for modernism that I'm trying to highlight in this debate, is that on the whole the ethnic, the cultural national community, which is such an important part of [Anthony Smith's] case, is rather like the navel. Some nations have it and some don't and in any case it's inessential. . . . So I would say there is a certain amount of navel about but not everywhere and on the whole it's not important. . . . The cultural continuity is contingent, inessential. [35: pp. 367, 369]

Concluding observations

Breuilly and Gellner's criticisms of ethnosymbolism undoubtedly point to the central issue in the debate about the relationship between pre-modern forms of group consciousness – whether we describe these using terms such as ethnicity/ethnic groups or national identities/nations – and modern nationalism. The question is, however, whether their argument holds water – or rather, to what extent. It seems to me that their general point – that it is difficult to establish a causal link between pre-modern nations/national identities and the modern nation-state/nationalism – is persuasive. It is one thing to identify proto-national forms of identity and loyalty that had formed before the eighteenth century. It is quite another to correlate the successful transition to nation-statehood of certain societies – England, France, the Netherlands, Sweden, Switzerland – to such cultural and symbolic antecedents. It is indeed difficult to attribute the genesis of nationalism and early nation-state-hood to the objective importance of such myths and symbols. Equally important is Breuilly's insistence on the essential role of institutions in forming and consolidating collective identities within large territories and over long time spans.

What is disputable is Breuilly's claim – which is also implicit in Gellner's theory – that what distinguished pre-modern ethnic patterns from modern nations is that the former were non-institutional. Breuilly's restriction of institutionalised identity to the modern period results from his equation of national institutions with the institutional apparatus of the modern nation-state: above all, an education system, a common legal code and an institutionalised public culture. We may accept without hesitation that these genuinely modern institutions are essential to spreading a sense of nationhood from a small educated elite outward to the public at large. But, at least in principle, pre-modern institutions could fulfil the same function, if perhaps somewhat less effectively than the modern nation-state. Nor are the church and the dynasty, as far as their normative outlook and political aims are concerned, necessarily irreconcilable with ethnic or national forms of identification and loyalty.

Breuilly's point about the conflicting visions of religious and national identities undoubtedly applies where the Reformation led to deep and sustained religious divisions. It holds water for German Catholicism, or for Swiss political Catholicism for that matter. The *Kulturkampf* of the 1870s in both countries offered a clear indication that the Catholic Church was opposed to the secularising nation-state [44: pp. 100–1; 53: ch. 1; 22]. But in several other pre-modern societies, including England and the Netherlands, as well as in Catholic ones like Poland, Ireland and France, religion in general and the church in particular often functioned as an incubator of national sentiment, particularly where religion served as a vehicle to accentuate national differences. In fact, both church and dynasty could be significant institutional carriers of the kind of cultural bonds (language, religion, symbols, communal narratives) that would come to lie at the heart of modern nations and the nation-building efforts of the nationalising state [27: p. 24; 40: pp. 67–73; on France, 24: chs. 1 and 6; on Britain, see 30 and 29].

Nor should we quickly discard as non-institutional and therefore irrelevant what Hobsbawm calls 'proto-nationalism', embodied in memories of former statehood and the concept of a political 'historical nation'. To be sure, such proto-nationalisms are not the same as modern nationalism. Both in terms of their 'ideological quality' (the demands for popular sovereignty and self-determination were usually absent) and their social and political scope (their appeal was frequently confined to the literate elites) there are significant differences. The assumption of strict continuities between proto-nationalism and modern nationalism is therefore highly questionable in most cases.

The same caution is warranted with regard to alleged continuities between pre-modern manifestations of patriotism and modern national-ism. 'Patriotism' – whether defined as 'love of country' or 'loyalty to one's fatherland and institutions' – undoubtedly represents a sentiment much older than nationalism. But certainly before 1800 (from the late nineteenth century onwards 'patriotism' was frequently used as a counter-term to 'nationalism') such sentiments were often focused on a particular town or region rather than on an entire 'nation'. Nationalism was not simply a continuation of patriotism with other means, although in late eighteenth-century Europe the two movements were closely inter-linked [on patriotism as a historical phenomenon, see 54: ch. 1; 45: pp. 23–7; 24; 55: ch. 3].

Even so, as Hobsbawm insists, where memories of former statehood existed they 'made the task of nationalism easier . . . insofar as existing symbols and sentiments or proto-national community could be mobi-lized behind a modern cause or a modern state' [40: p. 77]. Such mem-ories of pre-modern statehood aided the mobilisation of a number of national movements, including those of Hungary, Poland, Russia, Bohemia, Greece and Serbia. In some cases, these patriotic memories were confined to relatively small elites. Yet in other cases – certainly in Poland, Russia and Bohemia – they were kept alive by what might be regarded as the most powerful of all pre-modern institutions: church and priesthood. Even in the case of Zionism, memories of ancient statehood and exile, which for centuries had played a central part in the Jewish religious and liturgical tradition, played a key role in the construction of a highly effective nationalist idiom.

Nor was it irrelevant whether the demands of national movements – whether in the shape of claims for increased political participation within the empire, calls for autonomy, or demands for outright self-determination – could be credibly justified on the grounds of former statehood. In fact, the ability to do so could improve the status of the movement both internally and externally. As Miroslav Hroch has noted: 'It was an advantage if the national movement could present its demands for participation or for autonomy as a continuation or reconstruction of an old but partially oppressed statehood, as was the case for the Poles, Magyars, Czechs, Norwegians and Croatians' [Hroch in 14: p. 78; see also 41]. Late nineteenth-century nationalists, as well as the ideological protagonists of the successor states established after the First World War, would build on memories of former statehood to mobilise their populations, and to gain external recognition for their projects. These themes will concern us in the next two chapters.

2 Towards the Mass Nation: Nationalism, Commemoration and Regionalism

Let us now turn from the conceptual and historiographical to the history of nationalism in the late nineteenth and early twentieth centuries. One of the distinctive features of this period of European history was the transformation of nationalism into a mass phenomenon. As mentioned in the last chapter, in the early nineteenth century (at least before the revolutions of the 1840s) nationalism had in large part been the preserve of the educated middle classes. It was not until the last third of the century that the concept of the nation – with its constitutive notions of cultural authenticity, historicist growth and political self-determination – began to capture the imagination of the wider public and became a key mobilising force in the modern political arena. It was during this period of European history that nations became mass communities affecting the lives of hundreds of thousands, if not millions, of people. If we wish to explain why both in 1914 and then again during the inter-war period, national solidarities proved on the whole superior to class solidarities, then part of the answer has to be sought in this transformation. This chapter discusses some of the causes and consequences of this transition, focusing mainly on western and central Europe. In the next chapter the focus will shift towards an exploration of anti-imperialist and (after the First World War) state-building nationalism in east-central Europe.

The rise of the modern mass nation: nationalism and political culture

Two developments played a key role in the popularisation of nationalism before and after the First World War: the increasing importance of the nationalising state, and the national mass rituals and commemorative festivals that became such a conspicuous feature of Europe's public space. Both developments constitute essential ingredients of the history of nationalism in the period under consideration; they are also intimately linked. Thus the rise of the nationalising state in western and central Europe in the closing decades of the nineteenth century, allied as it was with the extension of democratic participation, reinforced public interest in the commemorative festivals and celebrations that became such an integral feature of Europe's political landscape.

Yet the undisputed power of the modern nation-state and its cultural policy notwithstanding, modern nationalism was no one-way street. This has been demonstrated by a number of innovative recent studies of the relationship between regional and national identities. Regions and localities did not merely passively receive national messages sent out from the centre but actively contributed to the nationalist project. In doing so, they shaped the ways in which, for example, national festivals were organised, carried out, perceived and debated in the national and local press.

The discussions in this chapter will be linked to two broader issues that over recent years have emerged as central to the study of nationalism. The first concerns the role of certain key actors in fostering national awareness, particularly the interplay of the national state and its personnel on the one hand, and of civil society on the other. The second relates to the links between politics and culture, and between deliberate nation-oriented activity and the ways in which the nation was symbolically represented.

The nationalising state: building institutions, fostering national culture

By the close of the nineteenth century, much of Europe – with the significant exception of its eastern and south-eastern regions, which were still in the grip of large empires – was divided into nation-states. Thus if, following John Breuilly, we regard nationalism primarily as a political ideology employed in struggles over the control of the state [28: p. 1], then the following question arises for central and western Europe after Italian and German unification: did nationalism still have a role to play once its key objective – the establishment of an independent state – had been accomplished?

The answer to this question must be a unanimous 'yes' – for two reasons. The first has to do with the ideology of modern nationalism.

Most nationalists – irrespective of whether they subscribed to a voluntarist conception of nationhood, where the stress is on an individual's identification with a set of political and cultural values, or regarded the nation as a community of shared ethnic descent – perceived themselves as engaged in a project that went beyond the creation of an independent state and included the creation of a culturally and institutionally integrated territory. Almost invariably, the proponents of the modern, secular state therefore regarded a high degree of unity – whether in terms of language, cultural values, political institutions or ethnic composition – as eminently desirable. The second reason concerns geopolitics: most so-called nation-states (including, which tends to be forgotten, modern France) lacked the degree of linguistic and cultural homogeneity that would have satisfied nationalist ambitions, and some (like Germany) even included substantial ethnic and national minorities [see 66: chs. 2, 4, 5].

The combination of these two factors – the relative lack of ethnolinguistic and/or institutional homogeneity and the nationalist belief in its desirability – constitutes the root cause of the phenomenon that John Breuilly has described as 'nation-building nationalism' and Rogers Brubaker has termed the 'nationalising nationalism' of the majority group within the state [28: p. 288; 64: p. 5]. It is from this incongruity of reality and ambition that flew a host of techniques and strategies, ranging from projects of institutional penetration and cultural policy to forced assimilation, expulsion, and worse. It is no accident that the means adopted by nationalists became more aggressive and extreme in the wake of the geopolitical turmoil of the First World War and the large minority populations it created particularly in eastern Europe – a theme that will concern us in the next chapter.

But even in more advanced western and central Europe, state authorities and their supporters pursued their nation-building agenda with a considerable degree of vigour and aggressiveness. This included the administrative and political penetration of the national territory through common legislation, policing and tax collection. But it went much further than that. In European societies such as Britain, Germany, France, Italy, Sweden and Switzerland, the state 'undertook major civilian functions, sponsoring communications systems, canals, roads, post offices, railways, telegraph systems, and, most significantly, schools' [82: p. 730; see also 71: pp. 116–21, 209–21, and the various contributions in 93]. This modern infrastructure was designed to bring large numbers of people in contact with the state and at the same time to foster a standardised national mass culture. It was largely through such state-induced policies that nationalism was transformed from a peripheral ideological movement into an institutionalised 'common sense' [62]. The process is well captured by Eric Hobsbawm:

> In the course of the nineteenth century these interventions became so universal and so routinized that a family would have to live in some very inaccessible place if some member or other were not to come into regular contact with the nation state and its agents: through the postman, the policeman or gendarme, and eventually through the schoolteacher . . . Government and subject or citizen were inevitably linked by daily bonds, as never before. And the nineteenth-century revolutions in transport and communications typified by the railway and the telegraph tightened and routinized the links between central authority and its remotest outposts. [40: pp. 80–1]

A closer look at France and Germany can help to illustrate these developments. The best research on the institutional aspects of modern nation-building deals with France, reflecting that country's strong centralist tradition and sustained concern with public mass culture. Eugen Weber's book *Peasants into Frenchmen* (1976) provides a particularly impressive example of this genre. Weber meticulously investigates the Third Republic's efforts to nationalise rural France – through the building of roads and railways, state-induced history and language education, military conscription, and through the democratic political process [97; for a concise summary of his argument, see 98: pp. 159–88]. Weber's account is inspired by modernisation theory, and his dense and nuanced argument therefore fits rather well with Gellner's structural–functional theory of nationalism. Weber argues that certain (economic) needs increased the pressure on the state to create a uniform (language-based) high culture within the existing state territory. Once this was in place, more and more people 'learned to appreciate the possibilities that went with the new scale of national operations and the objectives of the national state' [99: pp. 289–90].

According to Weber, the residents of France lived in different historical time zones until the authorities of the Third Republic launched a massive project of cultural standardisation. Originating in the great cities, the project subsequently spread outwards to the remotest provinces. The consequence was a reduction of the gap between the relatively advanced metropolitan centres and the rather backward rural areas, which had hitherto been only marginally integrated into the French nation-state. Through a revolution in transport and communication, rural France became part of a common national market and a public sphere, enabling French peasants to conceive of themselves as forming part of the French nation-state.

Elementary education played an even more prominent role in this process. In 1881, true to republican spirit, all fees and tuition charges in public elementary schools were abolished. In 1882, enrolment in a public or private school was made compulsory, and one year thereafter every village or hamlet with more than 20 school-age children was required to maintain a public elementary school. In 1886, an elementary teaching programme was instituted, along with elaborate provisions for inspection and control [97: p. 309; for authors who have challenged Weber's argument, see, for example, 68; 81]. Geography and history were added to a school curriculum that had hitherto centred on religious instruction, grammar, drawing and music.

At the centre of the nationalising programme, however, was language instruction. The authorities' great efforts in making French the uncontested language of the Republic were not just because it provided a precondition for mass communication and social mobility, but also because it served as a symbol of French national unity. The Third Republic's official mission was still that of the one and indivisible nation, and this inevitably meant that linguistic diversity was largely seen in negative terms [97: ch. 6]. Given that, even as late as 1870, French was the active language of no more than half of France's population, there was still much left to be done from the point of view of republican nationalists. Over a million of France's inhabitants spoke Breton in the 1880s, and there were still numerous speakers of Basque, Flemish, German dialects, Catalan, and so on [94: p. 304; 97: ch. 18). The persistence of linguistic diversity is a strong indication of the strength of regional identity in France at the turn of the century and beyond.

The inhabitants of rural France had several motives to learn French. One was that the new idiom carried prestige. In his vivid recollection of his childhood in inter-war Brittany, for example, Pierre-Jakez Hélias wrote that parents 'aspired to having their children sanctified by the elementary-school diploma, which would be framed and hung nobly on the front of the cupboards, between the pious images and the photographs of family weddings'. Another reason why parents displayed such a 'resolute desire' to have their offspring 'learn the language of the bourgeoisie' was the constant humiliation that non-French speakers were facing: those who had gone to Paris 'to earn a living soon began to

31

hate their own language, which to them was not only synonymous with poverty, but a symbol of ignorance and an assurance that they would be mocked' [77: pp. 151–2].

While post-unification Germany did not possess France's tradition of state centralism, the German lands too witnessed a dramatic extension of the communication infrastructure that had existed before 1871. The railway network, which had been begun in the 1840s, was rapidly expanded after unification. In 1870 the entire network consisted of about 19,000 kilometres of track. By 1910 it had grown to 61,000 kilometres [Berghahn in 63: 171]. All this contributed to alteration in people's sense of time and space, in their ability, in Benedict Anderson's phrase, to imagine the nation. The same holds true for popular education. German state authorities, it is true, did not have the power to introduce a single national curriculum along French lines. Even so, both political authorities and the educated middle classes successfully endeavoured to expand the system of public education and to improve the skills of the teaching personnel, with considerable consequences. School attendance was at approximately 90 per cent in 1871, rising to almost 100 per cent after 1880. The average national literacy rate was 87 per cent in 1871 – it was considerably higher in the Rhine provinces and much lower in eastern Prussia – rising towards 100 per cent by 1890. What is more, particularly in elementary schools the 'nation' came to play a prominent role. New subjects such as history, geography and language education gained in weight at the expense of traditional ones, notably religious education. In the *Gymnasium,* the grammar schools that prepared the German elite for careers in the civil service or the free professions, history and geography became more important than Latin and Greek. A new spirit of patriotic education – *vaterländische Erziehung* – began to be noticeable in all areas of public education, from religion to language instruction to history [for details, see 100: pp. 1191–209].

Nationalism in the age of mass politics

The undisputed significance of state-driven institution-building notwithstanding, however, nationalism was a project with many participants. The path towards the modern mass nation was not, at any rate, tantamount to a process of institutional penetration and cultural diffusion. Nor can it be satisfactorily analysed in terms of a state-induced endeavour at ideological manipulation. Rather, the process by which men and women of different social classes were drawn into a modern public sphere and became engaged with national institutions was in large part a consequence of the increasing politicisation of public life. All over Europe, the expansion of social communication and the extension of popular education was thus closely interwoven with an expansion of democracy and the formation of political parties. These developments provided the structural conditions for the nation-wide debates over public institutions and political culture – over schools and education, over roads and railroads, over national symbols and matters of foreign policy – that became such a conspicuous feature of modern society.

To be sure, the nation-state was decisive as an institutional frame of reference. Rephrasing Max Weber's famous dictum, one might argue that the modern nation-state supplied the cognitive and normative cage in which the struggles over politics and culture were played out. Its immediate effect was to channel public debate over institutions and symbols along 'national' lines. Because the champions of the nation-state pursued their agenda in the name of the nation, those who opposed it could no longer afford to justify their grievances by reference to sectional interests and preoccupations alone. Equally important, the nation-state also became a source of status and prestige for its constitutive parts. The historical regions and localities, which will concern us further below, began to compete for status, prestige and recognition within this new frame of reference – not just for economic resources and political influence. They began to stress their past and present contributions to the nation and its institutions. They were eager to claim a role for themselves within the life of the nation-state, and to receive recognition for it. But the aims and ambitions of these groups were often contested in the public sphere, reflecting the great variety of interests and ideas prevalent in society. Depending on their religious or regional affiliation and their position in the occupational and class structure, people subscribed to different visions of the nation.

The rise of modern mass democracy, which affected all of western and central Europe in this period, demonstrates that the nationalisation of the masses was the result of an interplay between state-induced nationalism and the nation-oriented activity fostered within civil society. Universal suffrage and the proliferation of newspapers accelerated the amalgamation of local and national political life still further and thus helped transform nationalism from a middle-class into a mass phenomenon. The rise of mass democracy inaugurated a new era of party politics. The notable politics of the early nineteenth century began to give way to a contest among rival parties and political pressure groups [on this European trend see 78: ch. 4; 72: chs. 11 and 14]. In this new political climate, success could no longer be taken for granted but was to become the reward for intense and deliberate political activity. To be successful, parties and leading politicians had to pay more attention to the development of political strategies and ideological messages that could appeal far beyond the confines of a particular milieu or class. In Germany, for example, the 'force of public opinion had ... grown tremendously since Bismarck's day' due to the rapid and powerful expansion of the political press and the propagandistic efforts of nationalist pressure groups [90: p. 77; see also Lerman in 63]. This applies with equal, if not greater, force to the France of the Third Republic, with its assemblies and elections, its parties and pressure groups, and its dense and wide-ranging network of newspapers, associations and political parties [on France, see 94: pp. 97–130].

Most crucially perhaps, within the institutional framework of the developed nation-state most political conflicts and controversies became infused with nationalist rhetoric. Nationalism provided the most powerful source of moral authority – and thus of political mobilisation – for those wishing to gain political recognition and success. Thus conflicts over politics tended to take the form of struggles over the definition of national identity. Nationalism became an integral part of political culture.

In France, the Dreyfus affair of the 1890s and subsequent controversies over foreign policy offer a clear testimony to the political significance of nationalist argument [94: pp. 462–7; 98: ch. 9; 101: ch. 9]. In Germany, meanwhile, the state-induced *Kulturkampf* against German Catholicism, the anti-Semitic agitation of the 1870s and 1880s, and the anti-socialist legislation against the alleged threat from the Left are manifestations of nationalism's exclusionary tendencies towards cultural and political minorities. In different ways and for different reasons that cannot be explored here, all these groups were perceived as posing a threat to the internal unity of the nation, its culture, and its normative and institutional order. The controversy over the enlargement of the German army of 1887 provides another example of this intimate fusion of nationalism and politics. When the Reichstag accepted a three-year term rather than the Septennat (Bill) Bismarck had requested, Conservatives, Free Conservatives and National Liberals launched a campaign against the Left Liberals and Social Democrats, brandishing them as anti-patriotic. [On Germany more generally, see 61: pp. 96–110;

on German nationalism and the *Kulturkampf,* see 53: ch. 1 and 56: pp. 56–8; on France, see 72: 333.]

Inter-nationalist competition: nationalism and imperialism

But nationalism cannot be explained by reference to the domestic political arena alone. The interrelationship of domestic and international developments provides a key to our understanding of national identity. Once nationalism established itself as the dominant political force in nineteenth-century Europe, it was bound to stir up competition among different conceptions of nationality and to serve as a major catalyst of national self-assertion. Thus one of the major driving forces of European nationalism in the period from 1890 to 1940 was inter-nationalist competition. The revolutionary upheavals and wars of the nineteenth century had confirmed the significance of international and geopolitical factors in stimulating national sentiment. After the Compromise Agreement of 1867 between Austria and Hungary and after German and Italian unification, this process intensified further. Around 1900, at the height of European imperialism, nationalism became even more fiercely competitive, reaching a new fever pitch during the inter-war period.

One area in which this new competitive nationalism manifested itself was the arts. Thus in 1896 an executive member of the Swiss National Museum identified a pervasive European nationalism as the prime cause of altered trade patterns in national antiquities:

> It is not least in the great art auctions that a phenomenon has become visible that has hitherto been confined to the sphere of politics. The trade in antiquities has become affected by a national movement insofar as every country endeavours to buy their own pieces of art. Whereas in the past the English or French used to buy anything they liked in other countries, irrespective of the origin of an object, there has been a clear shift in both England and France towards [national] antiquities, even in those cases where these are undoubtedly of a lower artistic value than available foreign ones. The Englishmen tend to buy the English, the Frenchmen the French, the Germans the German, and the Belgians and Dutchmen the Dutch old works of art. This is not true merely of historical museums but also applies to private collectors. [55: p. 197]

In larger and more powerful states, this preoccupation with an authentic national culture was often linked to imperialist visions of national grandeur. In post-unification Italy, for example, the architect

Camillo Boito urged his professional colleagues to attempt to develop a truly 'national style', which was currently visible in many of Europe's big cities. Italy, he concluded, had to follow their example by fostering a truly national style that would invoke Italy's great past. As he posed the problem in the 1880s:

> Nations are already searching for a style: the Germans return to their ogival style, the English to their Tudor, the Russians hold on to their Byzantine, the French are undecided between their Gothic and their Renaissance style. For Italy, the marvellous richness of its past constitutes its greatest obstacle. But sooner or later, an Italian architectural style will have to emerge, especially now that Italy has become a nation, and has its capital. [Tobias in 19: pp. 171–2]

But it was in the antagonism between France and Germany that the fusion of nationalism and imperialism found its clearest expression. Public buildings and monuments like the Eiffel Tower, constructed for the Exhibition Universelle of 1889 in commemoration of the centennial of the French Revolution, provide good illustrations of this trend. As a monument of outstanding proportions, the Eiffel Tower was to convince the rest of the world that France, a nation with a great and venerable past, was at the same time a forward-looking country with a great future. This was particularly important at times of crisis and humiliation, when French society felt threatened in its status and prestige. For many, it was a step towards France's regaining confidence after the domestic turmoil and military defeat of 1870/71. To quote from a particularly bellicose statement directed against the big neighbour across the Rhine:

> Bow down, Teutons: here is the marvel
> Unlike any other in the world.
> For Teutons, it is France that holds the torch
> That brings light to the smallest hamlet.
> [Loyrette in 89, vol. 3: p. 361]

Inter-nationalist competition also provided a motive for educational efforts by historians. The role of prominent scholars like Heinrich von Treitschke (1834–96), Max Weber (1864–1920) and Theodor Mommsen (1817–1903) in shaping the national consciousness of Germany's educated middle classes is well documented. In France, historians were much more directly involved in the state's project of mass education. The French historian Ernest Lavisse (1842–1922), for example, the author of the famous basic history textbook popularly known as the *Petit*

Lavisse, named the return of Alsace as one of the prime inspirations for his own educational mission:

> Since that dreadful year [1870–1] I have never for one minute given up hope. I have tirelessly preached that hope, and the confidence I feel, to millions of children. I have said that we have a permanent duty to the lost provinces, and repeated it often. Strasbourg's spire has never vanished from my horizon. To me it has always stood apart, soaring heavenward: 'I am Strasbourg, I am Alsace, I salute you, I am waiting.' [89, vol. 2: p. 161; on the German–French antagonism between 1870 and 1918, see also 79: chs. 3–5; see also 74]

It is sometimes argued that, from around 1890, imperialism replaced nationalism as the prevalent ideological movement. This view is rather misleading. It would be more accurate to say that nationalism and imperialism became fatally and inextricably linked, mutually reinforcing each other. In the large and powerful states at least, committed nationalists were usually champions of imperialist projects because they believed that the honour of their nation depended on success in the race for empire. Joseph Chamberlain in Britain, Jules Ferry in France, and Heinrich von Treitschke and Max Weber in Germany were in complete agreement that the future of their nations depended on their abilities to build large colonial empires. Eminent sociologist and liberal nationalist Max Weber, for example, had always insisted that the unification of Germany had set his country, quite inevitably, on an imperialist course. Thus in 1916, Weber argued that 'wars for power' were unavoidable 'for the foreseeable future' because 'the preservation of national culture is linked necessarily to power politics' [84: p. 65]. To be sure, neither in France nor Germany did the proponents of imperialist foreign policy remain unchallenged. While French revanchists opposed Jules Ferry's colonial ambition as a distraction from regaining Alsace-Lorraine, some German nationalists saw a large navy-building project as a competitor for resources with a more powerful army. Still, from 1900 onwards it became increasingly difficult to publicly oppose calls for imperial expansion. 'Imperialist policies', Wolfgang Mommsen has emphasised, 'were looked at from this vantage point as a source of strength to the nation, not only in terms of power and economic resources, but also in moral terms' [85: p. 219; see also 72: pp. 334–43].

Given that the stakes and expectations were invariably high, the persistent frustration of imperialist objectives tended to reinforce nationalism, rendering it potentially aggressive and expansionist. This was hardly a problem for Britain with its extensive imperial possessions. France too had been relatively successful in the imperialist race. Of the major European powers it was above all Germany which saw its hopes for imperial grandeur, fuelled since 1890 by the ambitious Kaiser Wilhelm II, thwarted on several occasions. This led to serious misgivings and a profound sense of crisis at home. Thomas Nipperdey judged the impact of imperial failures on the public mood in Germany around 1900: 'If the other great powers become world powers and the Germans remain confined to the Continent, then the Germans are threatened by a loss of power, even destruction' [88: p. 598]. Failures on the imperialist front were frequently explained as a consequence of national degeneration and crisis, which tended to be blamed on the 'enemies within', with Jews, Catholics and socialists constituting the preferred scapegoats [88: pp. 595–609; 72: pp. 340–1].

This close interrelationship of imperialism and nationalism was not confined to the political sphere but manifested itself in various areas of public life, including sports and national ritual, as well as high and popular forms of art. A few examples must suffice. The author of an article that appeared in *Le Temps* in July 1888 advocated the introduction of sport in schools, but fiercely opposed the idea of foreign imports: 'Let us be French; let us be so passionately, even in little things; let us be so above all in weighty matters like the education of our sons, if we want France to survive in the midst of the wild beasts that roar around it' [98: p. 213]. International sport became popular, providing new opportunities for representing national identity in a competitive way. The period between the 1890s and the outbreak of the Second World War also saw the invention of a number of mass sports events that would attract international attention, including the Tour de France, the football World Cup, and the Olympic Games. Hobsbawm explains the emotive appeal of football as an embodiment of national pride, drawing on his own experience as he listened to the football international between Austria and England while living in Vienna as a child in 1929: 'The imagined community of millions seems more real as a team of eleven named people. The individual, even the one who only cheers, becomes a symbol of his nation himself' [40: p. 143].

Worshipping the nation

Monuments, public festivals and commemorations

A glance at the cultural and symbolic sphere, and particularly at various forms of national ritual and commemoration, brings out even more clearly that by the end of the nineteenth century nationalism had begun to permeate the political culture of many European states. Although public festivals and commemorations had played a conspicuous role throughout the century, they became both more numerous and more extensive towards its close. Such nation-centred activity intensified as nationalism grew more competitive in the wake of German unification and as the imperial race was heating up between 1890 and the outbreak of the First World War. Different social actors, who embraced rival understandings of national identity, attended public festivals and commemorations. But what distinguished most national festivals and commemorations of the nationalist era was that the public was rarely confined to the role of passive bystander. Many played a part in the planning and organisation of these events, either through membership of private associations or through other forms of involvement in their local communities. Some even got involved as lay actors in historic plays or festival processions. [See the various contributions in 73; 55: ch. 5; 38: ch. 5.]

Let us look at a few examples. After the founding of the German nation-state under Prussian leadership in 1871, the annual military parades and commemorations played an important role in the overall attempt to buttress German national identity. From 1890, Wilhelm II endeavoured to foster a cult of his grandfather, Wilhelm I, and initiated the building of monuments to 'William the Great', particularly in Prussia. More successful were the so-called *Kaiserparaden,* which were held annually from 1876 in honour of the German emperor. As national mass rituals, they rapidly grew in importance after universal conscription had been introduced in Germany in the second half of the nineteenth century. While in Berlin and Potsdam these parades retained a predominantly elitist character until the First World War, in the provinces they were highly popular affairs. Here private associations rather than a close circle of military and political elites were responsible for organising the events, with the numerous war veterans' associations playing a particularly significant part. The parade in Leipzig in 1876 attracted more than 50,000 onlookers. The fact that the *Kaiserparaden* fused small-German militarism with monarchical symbolism undoubtedly enhanced their significance, because in doing so they appealed to the liberal movement that was sceptical of the monarchy but welcomed militarism as a symbol of national unity and strength. Monarchical symbolism, on the other hand, helped to make a Prussian-dominated German nation-state more acceptable to Catholics and those who would have favoured a (Greater-German) solution including Austria [96: pp. 68–9, 64; 65: chs. 2 and 3].

France witnessed a similar trend of state-induced nationalist activities in the closing decades of the nineteenth century. 14 July was declared a national holiday in 1880 in commemoration of the day in 1789 on which several thousand Parisians had taken the Bastille in the eastern part of the city. As in Germany, military symbolism played an outstanding role in French national self-assertion. The German notion of *ein Volk in Waffen* corresponded with the Third Republic's *une nation en armes,* with a big military parade forming the centrepiece of the annual 14 July celebrations [see 96: p. 204]. A similar process can be observed in Britain. It was at the height of this inter-nationalist competition that London was provided with a single administrative authority that subsequently converted the city, in the words of David Cannadine, 'from the squalid, fog-bound city of Dickens into an imperial city'. From the 1870s onwards, Disraeli and others were relentless and eventually successful in their efforts to transform the image of the monarchy. The latter institution, 'hitherto inept, private and of limited appeal', began to attract the interest of 'a broader cross section of the public than ever before' [Cannadine in 38: pp. 120, 123, 127].

The trend was pervasive. In 1900, a Swiss contemporary, looking back on three decades of intense commemorative activity, described the 'national festivals' as Switzerland's 'popular assemblies' and as the 'cults' that the Swiss 'consecrate to [their] Fatherland'. He concluded: 'If, in fact, we have become a people since the foundation of our new Confederation – and we have indeed – then we owe this to a large extent to the national festivals' [55: ch. 5]. This may sound like a highly optimistic assessment of the influence of public mass ritual on national integration considering that public festivals were never attended by a majority of the population. Yet we have to remind ourselves that, certainly in the industrialised societies, these events took place within a context of highly developed communication. The rise and rapid expansion of the popular press in the late nineteenth century undoubtedly increased the potential public impact of these events. Many of those who could not attend the central commemorative events, which tended to be staged in the larger towns, were either involved in simultaneously staged local festivals or followed them via reports in the press.

Of course, the large public festivals were frequently the site of fierce contestation rather than harmony. In Württemberg in the south of Germany, for example, many democrats and Catholics either did not participate in the Sedan Day celebrations or explicitly opposed the nationalist vision that the National Liberals associated with the holiday

[65: p. 73]. French national festivals and ceremonies were often equally contentious affairs, reflecting persistent class divisions as well as fierce conflicts between the Catholic Church and the champions of secular education or between the advocates of cultural assimilation and extreme nationalists [see the various contributions in 89, vol. 1]. Moreover, struggles over the interpretation of the national past emerged as a prominent feature of political discourse in many European societies in the late nineteenth century [see 98: ch. 1; 60; 102; 83].

Nevertheless, at least in the context of the developed nation-state, these public controversies had a shared – 'national' – focus or theme. National identities should not be equated with a consensus on core values but rather with a common preoccupation, engagement, even obsession, with the concept of the nation. The absence of such a consensus should not surprise historians given the great variety of cultural and political loyalties and interests within modern societies. This is why accounts are so unpersuasive that interpret the eruption of controversies over the public representation of nationhood – as embodied in debates surrounding the building of national museums and monuments or the staging of national festivals – as a sign that nationalism was ultimately insignificant.

This applies even more to national rituals that were performed during the large public festivals. Hundreds of thousands of people, many of them organised in private associations, took part in or at least observed such events: the raising of the national flag, the playing and singing of the national anthem, the performance of didactic historical plays, and so forth [see 38; 89; 73; 55: ch. 5]. Popular mass associations – the gymnasts, riflemen and singers – played a particularly important role in Germany, where after 1848 they constituted a pillar of a continuously expanding national movement. The members of these associations, through their activities, literally embodied what they considered the central national values and virtues [88: ch. 7; 75; 67; 70].

The aspect of active participation and involvement in national ritual – nationalism as concrete activity rather than abstract imagination – was even present where at first glance the main function was to represent the nation symbolically. The hundreds of monuments, statues and various works of art that began to populate the public space of large and small towns and villages all over Europe were designed to put the nation on permanent display. Yet as we shall see, many (perhaps the majority of) monuments and statues would not have been built if it had not been for the civic initiative and active collaboration of ordinary men and women.

41

Once erected and inaugurated, moreover, national monuments and statues were often (though not always) made a focal point of public festivals and commemorations [73].

The myth created around the German Chancellor Bismarck after his departure from office supplies a particularly instructive example [88: p. 599]. Between 1898 and 1914, more than 500 projects for honouring Bismarck's memory were initiated. Half of them were eventually realised. His memory was kept alive through public monuments and festivals, stamps and postcards, as well as painting and literature. According to one estimate, 166 Bismarck monuments had been erected in Germany by 1903, and by 1914 this number had risen to more than 500. Max Weber attributed Bismarck's elevation to the status of a national hero to the upper middle class's 'longing for a new Caesar' who would serve to inhibit socio-political reform and upward mobility – an interpretation that would later figure prominently in Hans-Ulrich Wehler's account of imperial Germany [cited in 76: p. 58; 100: pp. 849–53]. It may well be the case that Bismarck was seen as the charismatic leader and guarantor of autocratic stability against the forces of modernity. However, it was the Protestant public (and not the bourgeoisie or conservative power elite) that was responsible for the Bismarck craze. It was the more than 300 regional Bismarck societies, in which the petite bourgeoisie and university students dominated, that had initiated the boom in the construction of statues, towers, pillars and other kinds of monuments in his honour [100: pp. 849–54; 87: pp. 36–7].

It is their incorporation into cultural practice that renders the national mass rituals of the late nineteenth century more than mere symbolic representations or elements of society's cultural superstructure. Rather, they played a key role in fostering national identity and in turning nationalism into an ideological common sense. As we know from numerous newspaper reports and other public statements, participants in national festivals were often emotionally overwhelmed by the experience. This requires an explanation. One of the reasons why national rituals held such wide appeal may be seen in the fact that they literally embodied one of nationalism's distinctive characteristics – its self-referential quality. 'Nationalists', as John Breuilly observed, 'celebrate themselves rather than some transcendent reality, . . . although the celebration also involves a concern with transformation of present society' [28: p. 64]. The national festivals and commemorations are the purest manifestations of what has been the nationalist ideal ever since the French Revolution: 'a people worshipping themselves' [87: p. 2]. For the participants in the festivals, the nation ceased to be an abstract 'imagined community' and acquired the quality of a community of collective experience and sentiment. Yet as Mosse has noted, national rituals, quite apart from using liturgical forms, were not free of religious evocations. The appeal of national rituals appears to derive from their capacity to combine the tangibility of the face-to-face *Gemeinschaft* with the notion of sacral communion. Both elements reflect ideals that have been prominent in nationalist ideology: the nation as an extended family, and the promise of transcendence.

Commemorating fallen soldiers

We have already seen in the introduction that the First World War marked a watershed in the history of Europe. The way in which the war and the following peace settlement affected nationalism – particularly with regard to the treatment of ethnic and national minorities, and its relation to the rise of fascism – will concern us in more detail in chapters 3 and 4. But the First World War also provided the cause for nation-centred commemorative practices, and a few remarks on this topic are therefore appropriate at this point. Given that it profoundly affected the lives of millions of people, the war's central place in inter-war symbolism and iconography is hardly surprising. The seemingly archaic nature of trench warfare notwithstanding, this was the first war fought with the aid of modern technology and communication. Approximately 13 million soldiers were killed, which is about twice as many as in all major wars between 1790 and 1914 [86: p. 3]. Although the practice of commemorating the war dead was not invented after 1918, the First World War took it to new levels everywhere in Europe. 'The proliferation of monuments', so Antoine Prost explains the erection of some 38,000 monuments in inter-war France, 'reflected the depth of the nation's trauma' – the fact that 'virtually every family suffered at least one death' [Prost in 89, vol. 2: p. 308]. Official authorities often played a leading role in initiating and sponsoring projects designed to commemorate the war. But as we shall see in the next section, on nationalism and regionalism, this differed from country to country, reflecting different national traditions.

In an age in which the grip of religion in the traditional sense had markedly decreased, the logic and language of nationalism prevented these enormous losses from appearing utterly meaningless. Thus nationalism inspired what George Mosse has termed the 'Cult of the Fallen

Soldier'. Death was 'a sacrifice to the nation'. The cemeteries and the monuments built to commemorate the war dead – often combining classical and Christian themes and symbols – all came to serve the cult of the nation as a civil religion. As Mosse observed in his path-breaking study: 'The burial and commemoration of the war dead were analogous to the construction of a church for the nation, and the planning of such sacred spaces received much of the same kind of attention as that given to the architecture of churches' [86: pp. 32–3]. Once erected, these cemeteries and monuments became sites of national rituals whose content went far beyond the mourning of individual human loss. At their centre was the honouring of the ultimate sacrifice for the nation. In France, for example, the standard ritual on Armistice Day, 11 November, has remained the same to the present day. People congregate on their town or village square, where the names of the fallen soldiers are read out, followed by the sentence 'Mort pour la France' – fallen for France. As Antoine Prost has noted: 'Hardly a commune [township] in France is without a monument to the dead of that conflict' [Prost in 89, vol. 2: p. 307].

But there were also more trivial (though equally salient) forms of remembrance. The war became a theme of picture books and war novels, which were sold in tens of thousands in the 1920s and 1930s, many of which portrayed the war experience in rather romantic terms. More important still were the numerous war films that gained such great popularity in all the countries that had participated in the First World War. However, many of the films that appeared in the 1920s or early 1930s were realistic rather than romantic. Yet a pacifist film about the war like *All Quiet on the Western Front* (1930), based on Erich Maria Remarque's novel *Im Westen Nichts Neues*, was the exception. Even in the realistic films that were produced in France, Germany and England, there was much emphasis on the allegedly positive features of the war experience. As Mosse wrote: 'Even when any desire to glorify war was absent, it seemed impossible to avoid projecting ideals like camaraderie, courage, or sacrifice, which by their very nature endowed war with noble qualities' [86: p. 188].

Fascism – a movement that drew much of its leadership as well as its rank-and-file members from war veterans – capitalised on the war experience as it created its own rituals and symbolism and fostered its own *Weltanschauung*. But fascist leaders and their followers tended to keep aloof from official commemorative events, with the exception of Italy where fascists were in charge of the state shortly after the war. Things looked different in Germany, where throughout the 1920s the extreme right devoted all their energy to the destruction of Weimar democracy. Seeing themselves as an elite destined to fight mainstream bourgeois morality, the German National Socialists were eager to create and commemorate their own martyrs. The Munich putsch of 9 November 1923, in which Hitler and Ludendorff took part and in which 16 members of the movement were killed, provides a case in point. The National Socialists turned this failed attempt to remove the democratic Weimar regime into a commemorative day. During the 1930s, the 9 November death march 'emerged as the single most important event in the party's liturgical calendar' [59: p. 48]. Once in power, the Nazis gave the commemoration official status. The commemorative ritual included a speech by Hitler at the foot of the new monument for the fallen at the Feldherrnhalle, the singing of the Horst Wessel Song, and a parade past the crowds of Munich. The November commemorations were firmly in the hands of the party, leaving little scope for initiatives by private associations. But the evidence is that there was much 'spontaneous enthusiasm by great numbers of people who supported the Hitler regime' [59: p. 51]. Radio propaganda was used to bring the pageantry into the living rooms of hundreds of thousands, if not millions, of Germans, involving them in a ritual devoted to a mythology of blood sacrifice and national resurrection. And in 1936, the Nazis released a documentary film that explained the history and meaning of the 9 November march [59: pp. 53–4, 63].

The nation in the locality: nationalism and regionalism

We have already noted that official nationalism and related visions of national identity were often severely contested and subject to negotiation. There is no other field of investigation that has demonstrated this more than the study of nationalism in regional contexts, a field that has produced some of the most original works in recent years. The focus on how state-induced national projects were experienced in regional contexts has also contributed much to our understanding of the interplay of state and civil society. Rather than being passively received, state-sponsored initiatives elicited a host of responses from regions, localities, political parties and cultural associations. In the course of this process, official messages were redefined and to some extent transformed. Thus while traditionally regions have either been treated as empirical cases confirming larger structural trends (the approach of modernisation theory) or as bastions of opposition to such trends, the emphasis in much recent research in this field has concentrated on the interaction between nationalising state and different regional (as well as religious) interests and identities [see, for example, 65; 91; 53; 56; 95; 80].

It is from such regional studies that have emanated some of the most persuasive critiques of the equation of nationalism with a process of administrative penetration and cultural diffusion. Drawing on material from Württemberg in the period 1871–1914, Alon Confino has emphasised that the nation was effectively 'imagined' at the regional level; that it was above all in the German provinces that the success of official nation-building efforts was determined. It was in these localised contexts, Confino maintains, that the fate of elite-induced conceptions of 'Germanness', embodied, for example, in a military national festival like Sedan Day, was decided. Thus, if we are to gain a better understanding of the protean and contested nature of national identity – this is Confino's methodological message – we ought to conceive of the nation as a 'local metaphor' and concentrate on regional responses and perceptions rather than on the state's cultural policies. This would mean, moreover, that we give up the 'artificial dichotomy between nationalism from above and from below' and instead begin to explore 'nationhood as a process by which people from all walks of life redefine concepts of space, time, and kin' [65: p. 4; 57: ch. 1; for an overview of the literature, see 58].

In a stimulating chapter, Confino explores the impact of the Sedan Day celebrations on the population of Württemberg in the south of the German empire. Traditional historiographical wisdom had it that Sedan Day was at best a manifestation of the marked antagonism between a (southern) regional and (*kleindeutsch*) national identity, and at worst an example of a national holiday that failed. The reason for this harsh judgement was that it had never been officially embraced. Confino challenges this assertion through an examination of the attitudes that existed towards Sedan Day within civil society – political parties and private historical societies in particular. His analysis reveals that the Sedan Day celebrations, where they took place, were not conducted according to a fixed script and set of rules but according to the cultural tastes and historical traditions of local communities. 'Every community', Confino argues, 'was left to decide whether and how to celebrate' [65: p. 34]. The celebrations, although they were mostly initiated by the Protestant–liberal champions of the small-German nation-state and remained highly controversial among democrats, Catholics and socialists, were nonetheless significant because they brought the nation into the villages and small towns. Even those who opposed it took part in a debate over German nationhood. Many, perhaps the majority of people, came to celebrate a local festival. But once they took part they were exposed to the ideas of Sedan Day, and thus to the national idea.

Even in France, where the tradition of a strong centralist state lent added credence to the 'top-down' perspective of national sentiment, several historians, drawing on a variety of provincial examples, have questioned whether the metaphor of *Peasants into Frenchmen* was really adequate to describe nineteenth-century French society. James R. Lehning, for example, has recently concluded that historians should not attempt 'to find when and how peasants became French, but to discover the ways in which they served to define what being French meant, and the ways in which French culture defined what being a peasant meant' [81: p. 5]. Similarly, Caroline Ford, in her study of nationalism and regional identity in the Third Republic, insists that 'the creation of national identity is a process continually in the making rather than the imposition of a fixed set of values and beliefs' [68: p. 5; see also 69]. Focusing on the department of Finistère in Lower Brittany, Ford studies regional responses to the nationalising efforts of the French state during the last quarter of the nineteenth century. Specifically, she concentrates on the religious conflicts of the Third Republic. On the one hand, Ford's study confirms the commonly held view that the regional Catholic Church often provided a locus of resistance against the secularising nationalism of the French state. On the other hand, Ford also demonstrates that the church 'played an integrative role by mediating the cultural conflicts between center and periphery reconciling the nation with the region'. There emerged, she argues, a social Catholicism or republican clericalism that 'rejected the hierarchical, antirepublican politics by birthright while simultaneously voicing the legitimacy of the religious identity of the region'. In doing so, it offered a spiritual and political alternative to both the anti-clerical republican Left and the royalist Right. The social Catholic movement, Ford argues, endeavoured to 'bridge the political claims of the republican nation with the cultural claims of the region' [68: p. 6].

The memory of the war in the regions

Research on the First World War, and particularly on how the war dead were commemorated in different countries, has also thrown a new light on the dynamic relationship between official nationalism and local understandings of national belonging. There were clear differences between nation-states in terms of the part they played in defining standards for commemorative events, or in the planning and construction of war memorials.

In Britain, and particularly in France, state authorities were rather active and prescriptive in their approach to military cemeteries and monuments. The British War Graves Commission, founded as early as 1917, established firm rules concerning the design and care of military cemeteries. The Stone of Remembrance and the Cross of Sacrifice became the central ingredients of British military cemeteries of the inter-war period. In France, the Secretary of State for Front Line Veterans and Victims of the War played a decisive role as well. The state took a much less prominent role in Germany and Austria, a fact that Mosse attributes to a lack of financial resources in these two nations that suffered heavily from military defeat and economic crisis. Yet although financial restrictions may have been partly responsible for the marginal role in the planning, building and maintenance of war cemeteries and memorials, they hardly provide a sufficient explanation. The low profile of the central state in Germany (at least before the creation of the Nazi dictatorship) also reflected the traditionally prominent part of private associations, regions and localities in German society. Associations such as the Volksbund Deutsche Kriegsgräberfürsorge played an extremely important role in this regard. In the area of monuments to the known and unknown dead, too, its legacy of regionalism meant that Germany lagged behind Britain and France. It was not until the late 1920s that Germany inaugurated its first big monuments to the war dead – the Tannenberg Memorial in East Prussia (1927) and the Tomb of the Unknown Soldier in Berlin (1931) – while the Cenotaph in Whitehall had been unveiled in 1920 [86: ch. 5].

But even in allegedly centralised France matters are less clear-cut than might be assumed. The voice of the provinces, and their contribution to constructing French identity, did not wane during the inter-war period. Daniel Sherman's illuminating analysis of the discourse and practice surrounding the planning and building of memorials to the war dead confirms this impression. In France – a country that suffered more than 1.3 million military deaths, which was more, in relative terms, than any other country – a 'commercial monument industry' developed immediately after the war. This caused concern among members of the central authorities and their aesthetic advisors, who subsequently sought to establish certain rules regarding aesthetic form and conformity. Educated members of provincial communes shared these worries. But while the large towns could afford to hire (often through competitions) artists who conformed to the aesthetic standards of the cultural establishment, the villages and smaller towns had to settle for mass-produced standard designs that could then be adapted to local tastes and needs. Interestingly, Sherman's study shows that the state authorities refused to interfere in the commemorative initiative of local communes, even where members of the local bourgeoisie tried to convince the state that the massive commemorative building wave cried out for central rules and regulations. In the summer of 1919 the Fine Arts Ministry replied as follows to a request, emanating from the local bourgeois establishment, for greater regulation: 'the ministry has abstained from intervening in the choice of artists in order to leave towns and [monument] committees the greatest scope for initiative' [Sherman in 73: p. 191; Prost in 89, vol. 2].

In this chapter we have focused mainly on nationalism as a force of institutional and cultural unification, despite the prominent part played by conflict and controversy in the politics of national identity. The geographical emphasis has been on the industrially developed nation-states of western and central Europe, above all Germany and France. The next chapter will lead us into what, in terms of the nature and role of nationalism, has sometimes been called a different time zone. It will lead us into eastern Europe, where the explosive dynamics of secessionist, homogenising and irredentist nationalisms were unleashed within a short space of time, with fateful consequences for ethnic and national minorities.

3 Boundaries of National Belonging: Nationalism and the Minorities Question

If in the large national mass rituals the stress was on communal loyalty and belonging, this should not prevent us from recognising that nationalism is as much about exclusion as it is about inclusion. While the prevalent nationalist doctrines varied from one society to another and were often fiercely contested, one of nationalism's most visible effects was to integrate by fostering the boundaries of national belonging. Nationalism fostered culture communities by supplying criteria for the definition of members as well as non-members. Whether we are focusing on a more liberal, 'Western' type of nationalism, where minorities are expected to assimilate to the culture of the majority, or on a more exclusivist variety, where cultural assimilation is considered difficult or even impossible – each version presupposes a core culture that is regarded as constitutive of the national community. The particular form nationalism adopted in a polity depended not just on cultural traditions and identities, but also, and even more so, on the political and geopolitical context in which it had to operate.

The rise of nationalism in the nineteenth century and its ultimate establishment as an internationally recognised political principle transformed the way in which both minority populations and imperial states were perceived. The view that distinctive cultural communities possess a legitimate claim to national self-determination – which, after all, is part of nationalism's doctrinal core – must almost inevitably lead to the politicisation of ethnicity. In central and eastern Europe at least – and well before the end of the First World War – it was the ubiquity of nationalism that transformed ethnic groups with no claim to independent statehood into 'nationalities' that harboured such claims. As Brubaker writes on the impact of nationalism on the Habsburg,

Ottoman, and Romanov empires in the second half of the nineteenth century:

> As the category 'nation' diffused eastward in the second half of the nineteenth century as a salient 'principle of vision and division' of the social world ... these imperial realms were increasingly perceived, experienced, and criticized as specifically multinational rather than simply polyethnic, polyreligious, and polylinguistic, and the 'principle of nationality' – the conception of states as the state of and for particular nations – became the prime lever for reimagining and reorganizing political space. [64: p. 3; see 126: ch. 7 for basic background on inter-war eastern Europe; on the collapse of empire and the identity crisis it provoked among the formerly dominant nationalities, see 118]

Brubaker's observation about nationalism's role in turning ethnic concepts into national ones is undoubtedly important and accurate. However, when it comes to examining the fate of minority populations during the inter-war period it is still useful to make a distinction between 'ethnic' and 'national'. The distinction, which is mainly contextual, can help us to sharpen our awareness that the situation of minorities in Europe differed (and still differs) in terms of the political possibilities open to them. Ethnic minorities were groups that did not possess a national homeland, as opposed to national minorities, which, at least theoretically, could migrate to, and expect protection from, their 'home' state. Examples of particularly large national minorities in inter-war Europe are the Hungarians in Romania and Czechoslovakia, the Germans in Poland and Czechoslovakia, and the Ukrainians and Belorussians in Poland. The classic example of an ethnic minority in inter-war Europe are the Jews, who, although they shared a sense of ethnocultural belonging, lived dispersed over several countries, including Poland, Russia, Germany, Hungary, Romania and Czechoslovakia. It was not until the founding of the state of Israel in 1948 that Jews could claim membership of a national state in which they formed the dominant group.

This chapter will highlight the relationship between nationalism and the aspirations of national and ethnic minorities. More specifically, it will examine the impact of 'state-building nationalism' – defined as attempts to 'assimilate or incorporate culturally distinctive territories in a given state' [114: p. 15] – on the plight of minority populations both before the First World War and during the inter-war period. The final section is devoted to an examination of the situation of the Jewish ethnic minority in east central Europe, particularly between the wars, and on the emergence of Zionism as a specifically Jewish nationalist response to such state-building nationalisms.

Nationalism and the treatment of minorities before the First World War

The vision of the one and indivisible nation in the West

Although the effects of state-building nationalism on minority populations became particularly visible during the inter-war period when a host of new nation-states sprang up from the ashes of three former empires in central and eastern Europe, the origins of the phenomenon lie in the last third of the nineteenth century. As discussed in the previous chapter, post-revolutionary France emerged as the pioneer of the assimilationist model of the one and indivisible nation, of the view, that is, which holds that national culture and state boundaries should be made to coincide. The state-building nationalism of the Third Republic, with its pressure on minorities to assimilate to the cultural mainstream, was rooted in a complex mixture of intellectual, structural and historically contingent factors. Ever since the Revolution of 1789, French republican nationalists had displayed a strong preference for unity over diversity. From the viewpoint of the revolutionaries, the new, unitary nation was to take the place of the immense diversity of the *Ancien Régime*. In part, this obsession with unity reflected the revolutionaries' philosophical conviction that only a culturally homogeneous nation represented progress, while diversity was a remnant of backwardness and superstition. At the time of the Revolution, French was the predominant language in only 15 of the nation's 89 departments. There were large population segments that spoke Flemish, particularly in the north, while Celtic was spoken in much of the west; Basque was frequently spoken in the south-west, while in the east, and particularly in the provinces of Alsace and parts of Lorraine, German was predominant [24; 115; 127].

But what is important to recall is that despite the salience of regional sentiment – what republicans derided as parochialism and particularism – at no time was the integrity of the French state seriously threatened by regional separatism. While the inhabitants of some regions in the south and west of France may have resented the French state and sympathised with a vision of cultural autonomy – a constellation that was clearly visible in Brittany – regionalism in France was on the whole not based on a concept of distinctive ethnicity or nationality. Nor did regionalist movements promote political independence from the centre. However dissatisfied individual regions may have been with the policies that emanated from Paris, the solution to the problem was seen within the framework of the French nation-state. In Robert Tombs's words: 'All the major political parties wanted to seize control of France and the State, not weaken or fragment it.' The French case raises, of course, the question of why such diversity, especially when under attack as during the Third Republic, did not respond with some kind of separatism. While there is no single answer to this question, a number of factors certainly played their part: France's uniquely strong republican legacy since the French Revolution, with its emphasis on cultural unity; the fact that this legacy was not only powerfully revived, but also institutionalised, during the Third Republic; and finally, we may point to the fact that ethnic minorities like the Bretons did not possess an external national homeland that could have supplied a nascent nationalist movement with the necessary ideological legitimacy and material resources [94: pp. 319–20].

The vision contested and reaffirmed: the Polish minority in Prussia

This was markedly different in post-unification Germany, particularly in Prussia with its substantial Polish minority. Of the total Polish population of 13.5 million in 1890, 6.9 million (51.1 per cent) lived in Russian-controlled Congress Poland, 3.7 million (27.5 per cent) in Austria (Cisleithania), and 2.87 million (21.3 per cent) in Prussia. The 2.87 million 'Poles' – people who in their majority 'spoke Polish or a related dialect' and who consided themselves members of the 'Polish nation' [88: p. 266] – made up approximately 5.8 per cent of the German and 10 per cent of the Prussian population [90: p. 59; 138: p. 123].

While the Bretons and other regional groups in France may have defined themselves primarily as a cultural (and above all linguistic) minority, the Poles of eastern Prussia, especially after 1871, saw themselves as a separate nationality – as a group, that is, with a legitimate claim to an independent state. These claims had their roots in historical events predating German unification. In the eighteenth century, Poland–Lithuania was divided between Russia, Austria and Prussia. The division of Poland was condemned as an act of despotism by some of Europe's leading political thinkers – including Burke, Rousseau, Marx and Lord Acton – and the various Polish uprisings became a cause célèbre for European liberals and radicals throughout the nineteenth century. Yet while the division of Poland had led to the destruction of the Polish kingdom, it had not eradicated Polish national consciousness. On the contrary, the loss of the kingdom had reinforced Polish self-awareness, promoted chiefly by the Polish upper classes, the church, and subsequently the intelligentsia who acted as the guardians of Polishness throughout the nineteenth century [see 106: ch. 1; 129: pp. 28–9; on intellectual expressions of Polish romantic nationalism, see 135].

Polish national awareness was most strongly visible in Prussian Poland – in Poznania, Pomerania and Silesia. It was less marked in the more backward regions of Galicia and in Congress Poland. This was for several reasons. To begin with, this region had a relatively high concentration of members of the traditional Polish aristocracy and patriotic intelligentsia (Poznania, Pomerania) who showed a strong national awareness. Prussian Poland was also the most developed and dynamic part of the former Polish kingdom, confirming the close link between economic and cultural modernisation and nationalism. Silesia in particular was characterised by modern forms of agriculture as well as light and heavy industry. These advanced economic activities demanded a relatively well-educated workforce, which was reflected in the fall of illiteracy rates among the Polish population between 1870 and 1901 from 30 to 1 per cent. Some 65 per cent of the population were occupied in a modern form of agricultural production. There was fierce economic competition between Germans and Poles in this province. A Polish middle class emerged on a scale 'unknown in other parts of the partitioned country'. According to Wandycz, Prussian Poland became 'almost a Western-type province with many similarities, economic and social, to Bohemia' [136: pp. 177–9; 106: pp. 132–6].

Even more decisive in revitalising Polish nationalist aspirations was the repressive policy of the Prussian–German state against its perceived enemies. The motivations for this policy were complex rather than uniform, as were its manifestations. It ranged from measures designed to maintain traditional power relations, to religious discrimination, to forced assimilation and ultimately exclusion. Its main proponent was the nationalising secular state that had been created in 1871 and the nationalist pressure groups who supported it in its struggle against the alleged 'enemies' of the new *Reich*: the Catholic Centre Party during the *Kulturkampf* of the 1870s, the socialists, and, from the mid-1880s, the Poles of Prussia. The May Laws of 1873, which substituted German for

Polish in Poznanian secondary and elementary schools, were an early indication of this anti-Polish trend. In 1885, this was followed by the brutal expulsion of approximately 30,000 Poles and Jews (most of whom had lived in Prussia for generations but because they still lacked German citizenship possessed little legal protection from expulsion) to Russia and Galicia. From the 1880s onwards, a number of discriminatory laws, along with a state-sponsored settlement policy, were introduced to strengthen the position of German peasants vis-à-vis their Polish competitors and to stem the alleged 'Polonization of eastern Germany' [84: pp. 28–9; 112; 108; 138: ch. 6].

In 1886, Bismarck justified the expulsion from Prussian territory of Poles and Polish Jews carried out in the previous year in front of the assembled members of the Lower House of the Prussian Parliament. In his speech the German chancellor accused the Poles of having broken the trust that had once existed between the Prussian king and his Polish subjects. Fusing conservative-patriarchal with nationalist arguments, Bismarck questioned their loyalty to the Prussian state, which, he argued, had always treated them with respect. With the Warsaw rising of 1830 and the strong Polish contribution to the revolutionary uprisings in the 1840s this trust had been shattered. This had been despite the sympathies of most Germans, Berliners in particular, towards the Poles. The 'struggle for existence between the two nations', Bismarck concluded, was still waging unabated due to the activities of Polish nationalists and their Catholic German allies in the Prussian provinces. The Poles and those who supported their nationalist agitation (this was the gist of Bismarck's speech) posed a security risk to the Prussian state that could not be tolerated [see 117: pp. 173–86; for an authoritative account of German policies towards the Polish minority, see 102].

From the mid-1890s, these anti-Polish policies became more systematic and more openly nationalist. They also constituted the main cause for the formation of a number of voluntary associations that used anti-Polish rhetoric to mobilise support. The Pan-German League (founded in 1891) and the Society for the Eastern Marches (established in 1894) are important examples [108]. Many prominent German intellectuals supported an anti-Polish position. Wolfgang Mommsen's impressive account of Max Weber is particularly instructive in this respect. Before the First World War, Weber strongly opposed the Poles' calls for national autonomy, insisting that Germany had to pursue its civilising mission in the east of Prussia. Responding to accusations by the conservative Heinrich von Gerlach that the government's policy towards the Poles in imperial Germany was based on an excessive nationalism, Weber wrote in the organ *Die Zeit*: 'He deplores the repression of the Poles to second-class German citizens. But the contrary is true: we have turned the Poles into human beings' [84: p. 54]. In 1893, Weber joined the Pan-German League, and in 1894 he supported the League's Polish programme which called for the sealing of the eastern frontier to Polish migrant labourers and advocated a radical Germanisation of Polish culture in Prussia. If Weber began to adopt a more moderate line towards the Prussian Poles during the war – influenced by the work of Otto Bauer and other Austrian socialists, he now regarded Polish self-government and cultural autonomy as the way forward – this reflected his view of Germany's political interests rather than a genuine recognition of Polish rights. Weber was aware that the Prussian settlement policy had failed, and believed that gaining control over Poland was vital for Germany in its contest with Russia [84: pp. 53–6, 211–13].

State and nationality in Austria–Hungary after the 'Ausgleich'

Before moving to the inter-war period, the situation in the Habsburg Empire, where different national aspirations began to clash head on after the *Ausgleich* of 1867, will be outlined. The product of Austria's defeat by Prussia and of persistent Hungarian nationalism, this settlement led to the division of the Habsburg Empire into two multinational states: Austria (Cisleithania) and Hungary (Transleithania). Both states, the Austrian and the Hungarian, introduced new constitutions in which the status and rights of minorities were defined. Article 19 of the Austrian Constitution went as follows:

> All the races of the state shall have equal rights, and each race shall have the inviolable right of maintaining and cultivating its nationality and language.
>
> The State recognizes the equality of the various languages in the schools, public offices, and in public life.
>
> In the countries populated by several races, the institutions of public instruction shall be so organized that each race may receive the necessary instruction in its own language, without being obliged to learn a second language. [2: p. 156]

The Austrian Constitution of 1867 was a concession to nationalist pressures. It was not a declaration in favour of a federation of national-ities [137]. The leading exponents of the Austrian state understood them-selves as the members of an imperial *Hausmacht* rather than a nationalising state. 'Its *raison d'être*', to quote from Alan Sked's excellent account of the Habsburg Empire, 'was to provide a power base for the political ambitions of whichever Habsburg Emperor inherited it' [131: pp. 264–5; on symbolic representation of Habsburg authority after 1848, see Unowsky in 104]. But German culture continued to dominate official communication and institutions more or less as before 1867. This is not to deny that the Austrian Constitution was comparatively liberal in its conception of national minority rights. What created potential for conflict in practice, however, was that it was notoriously vague in answering a number of crucial questions: What constituted a nationality? What did national equality mean in practice? And, finally, who was responsible for enforcing the law?

This vagueness resulted in a protracted conflict over the interpretation of the constitutional arrangement on nationality rights. This became particularly visible in the increasingly fierce conflict between Czechs and ethnic Germans that raged in Bohemia and Moravia during the last three decades before the First World War. Both groups had developed a distinctive identity over past decades and indeed centuries. The first half of the nineteenth century had seen the rise of a Czech cultural nationalism, at least among the rapidly growing middle classes [see 41: pp. 44–5]. This trend was further accelerated in the second part of the century as a result of the combined effects of industrialisation, mass emigration and urbanisation in Bohemia and Moravia and of attempts on the part of the Austrian state to improve its administrative grip over its imperial provinces. Insofar as Czech nationalists like Palacky and Masaryk expressed their loyalty towards Austria, they did so mainly because they regarded the empire as a protector against German nationalist claims to the Bohemian lands. Once there was a prospect of Austrian weakness and German defeat, Czech calls for an independent state became stronger. As the later Czech president Masaryk argued in a memorandum in 1915: 'Austria, being an aggregate of nine small nations, is quite an artificial State . . . no nation in Austria is so populous that it would have the ruling majority' [cited in 130: p. 122].

The sense of identity of ethnic Germans living in Bohemia, on the other hand, was bound up with their historic status as a privileged minority in an imperial region where Czechs (or, rather, Bohemians) had for centuries formed the majority. They were determined to defend this position rather than making concessions to the Czechs in the name of Vienna's programme of political and cultural equality between the different nationalities. Conflict was almost unavoidable under these conditions, not least, as Sked has noted, because the vagueness of the Austrian Constitution left room for conflicting interpretations of 'national equality'. For the Czechs, national equality meant equal standing for the Czech language 'in communication with as well as within the public service', that schools should 'teach Czech to all Czech children', and that Czechs should occupy 'the same proportion of posts in the civil service as the proportion of Czechs in the relative population'. Referring to the same constitutional principle of national equality, the Germans insisted on keeping German as the only official language for German areas of Bohemia. The tensions between Czechs and Germans escalated in 1897, when the Austrian Prime Minister, Badeni, tried to win the Czechs' support by giving their language equal status with German as the language of administration in Bohemia and Moravia. This alienated the Germans even further from the Austrian imperial state and reinforced their pan-German convictions [131: pp. 230–5; documents on the language conflict between Czechs and Germans in the Bohemian parliament in 1902 can be found in 2: pp. 171–2].

Even in Austria itself, ethnic tensions became more marked in the decades before the outbreak of the First World War. In many Austrian cities that had experienced considerable ethnic immigration from the 1880s onwards – including Vienna, Graz, Salzburg, Innsbruck and Linz – a combination of assimilationist policies and active discrimination was designed to marginalise any languages other than German. In 1909 German was declared the only official language of government in Upper Austria [131: p. 225; 116: pp. 28–31; Beller in 104].

The official approach to the minority question was quite different in Hungary. Unlike the Austrian elite which acted as an imperial *Hausmacht,* after the Compromise of 1867 the Hungarian state began to develop a unitary nationalism on French republican lines. The Hungarian Nationalities Law of 1868 was inspired by the doctrine of the 'indivisible, unitary Hungarian nation'. Although it formally acknowledged the existence of different nationalities and made allowances for the use of the different languages spoken in the Hungarian part of the empire, the law was applied in such a way as to promote Hungarian language and culture at the expense of minority cultures. It came, in Sked's words, to be 'applied in such a way as to constitute an instrument of Magyarization' [131: p. 213]. Magyarisation – the cultural nationalism of the Magyar majority that dominated the state – was 'motivated by a sense of cultural superiority' on the part of the dominant group. Its impact was particularly marked in education, where the laws of 1879,

1883, 1891 and 1903 made Hungarian the official language in state and confessional schools. Another pillar of Magyarisation was electoral politics: Magyars took over 90 per cent of parliamentary seats, while Romanians, Slovaks and Serbs remained grossly under-represented. A law of 1898 determined that each town or village could have only one official (Magyar) name, to be approved by the Minister of the Interior. The tombstones of local cemeteries had to be engraved in Magyar [131: pp. 213–15; on the effects of Magyarisation, see also 120].

Not all minorities resisted Magyarisation. Portions of the German and especially of the Jewish educated classes showed a marked tendency to assimilate to Magyar language and culture. Provided they agreed to acculturate, Jews could play a significant part in Hungary's political and economic affairs. Under Tisza, they could enter the state bureaucracy and become cabinet members [131: pp. 210–11]. As Mendelsohn writes in his superb account of the Jews' plight in inter-war Europe, 'the Hungarian ruling class of the prewar period was uniquely open to the ideology of Jewish assimilation – more so, certainly, than was the German ruling class, not to mention the Romanian, Polish, or Czech elites' [122: p. 89]. Even so, Hungary's state-building nationalism caused considerable resentment among the economically and culturally less advanced ethnic minorities in the border areas. This applied in particular to the Slovaks and the Romanians of Transylvania. Yet with the exceptions of the Serbs and the Croats, none of these groups managed to launch a successful nationalist movement before the First World War [131: pp. 216–22].

State-building nationalism and the fate of national minorities between the wars

The First World War and the destruction of the German, Austro-Hungarian and Russian empires that it brought in its wake shifted the minority question to the centre of political attention. As the previous explorations have shown, the existence of minority populations within a region or state dominated by a particular ethnic group did not represent a new phenomenon – the Polish minority in the Prussian East or the Sudeten Germans in Bohemia spring to mind. Yet the creation of numerous new states on the principle of national self-determination dramatically increased the proportion of minorities in central and eastern Europe. Many of these states – and particularly Romania, Poland and

Yugoslavia – were as multi-ethnic or multinational as the empires that had vanished. Of the approximately 35 million minority inhabitants in inter-war Europe, only about one-quarter (i.e. around 8 million) lived in western Europe. More than 25 million lived in central and eastern Europe, and it is therefore only reasonable that a chapter on the relationship between nationalism and the minorities questions focuses on this region [121: pp. 55–6].

Many students of inter-war Europe have argued that, given the great number of minorities and of ethnically mixed areas in east central Europe, President Wilson's advocacy of national self-determination did inevitably spell disaster for the peace and stability of inter-war Europe [see, for example, 40: pp. 132–3]. While much can be said for this view, the heart of the problem was not so much the principle of national self-determination per se. As Miroslav Hroch has reminded historians:

> As an object of scholarly analysis, self-determination is neither 'good' nor 'bad'. Nor was the principle of national self-determination invented by President Wilson. In Eastern Europe, calls for self-determination had multiplied in the second half of the nineteenth century, albeit often inter-mingled with the somewhat weaker claim to national autonomy, in the national movements of the Poles, Hungarians and Czechs. This is not to deny that it was the collapse of the Austro-Hungarian, Russian and German empires in 1918 that lent an unprecedented force to these calls. [Hroch in 14: pp. 65, 81–2]

Yet the problem, rather, was the way in which dominant nationalities in the newly created states chose to interpret and apply the principle of national self-determination. In the Fourteen Points, Woodrow Wilson proclaimed that 'all peoples and nationalities' had a 'right to live on equal terms of liberty and safety with one another, whether they be strong or weak' [111: p. 113]. Yet as Hans J. Morgenthau wrote on the interpretation of these words in inter-war Europe: 'While men everywhere subscribed to the words of the Fourteen Points, it was particular nationalisms . . . that infused their particular meanings into these words' [125: p. 271]. Thus if the implementation of this principle in the new states led to conflict and instability, it was because most of the numerically dominant groups within them subscribed to a hegemonic (rather than federalistic) kind of nationalism that showed little regard for minorities or even regarded them as a threat to the nation-state. In this nationalist vision, the state had to be identical with the national culture of the majority, which was defined mainly in linguistic terms. Because none of the states created (or enlarged) after the war was homogeneous in ethnocultural terms, all of them, if to varying degrees – these policies were more marked in Poland and Romania than in Czechoslovakia, for example – witnessed state-driven cultural initiatives. Cultural autonomy, let alone political self-governance, was not tolerated within the state's territory. If minorities refused to assimilate, or sometimes even if they wished to retain their cultural identity, this was seen as a sign of disloyalty and a threat to the territorial integrity of the state [see 128: pp. 147–9].

While there is no denying that this integral nationalism was morally objectionable, it was fuelled, at least in part, by the irredentist nationalism of those states that had been militarily defeated. Thus the biggest benefactors among the successor states – Poland, Czechoslovakia and Romania – came immediately under pressure from the major revisionist states – particularly Germany and Hungary, but also Russia – who sought to revise the territorial status quo. The armed clashes that followed the Armistice in 1918 and in some cases lasted until the early 1920s, among Poles, Ukrainians and Russians in Galicia, between Germans and Poles in Upper Silesia, between Romanians and Ukrainians in the Bukovina, between the Hungarian Red Army and the troops of the new Czechoslovak Republic and of Romania provided an early manifestation of the vicious circle unleashed by geopolitical turmoil, the nationalism of the new states and the revisionist ambitions of the defeated and territorially reduced states. This 'generalized Central European civil war of the immediate postwar years' provided a foretaste of the 'barely controlled enmities of the interwar period' [107: pp. 132–3].

Thus hegemonic nationalism, aimed as it was at cultural homogenisation through either forced assimilation or expulsion of minority populations, was in part a response to irredentist pressures. To acknowledge this is not to justify the kind of nationalism practised by the authorities of the newly created states: re-emergent Poland, Czechoslovakia, and massively enlarged Romania. In all of these states one nationality was dominant demographically and politically (though in the case of Czechoslovakia demographic majority was only achieved by constructing the hybrid nationality of 'Czecho-Slovaks'), yet all were composites of nationalities rather than nation-states in the strict sense [see statistical tables in the Appendix]. To be sure, there were attempts after the war to protect the rights of minorities. All in all, 14 agreements regulating the treatment of national and ethnic minorities were concluded between

1919 and 1923 between the Allied and Associated Powers and the states whose populations included substantial minority populations. These were Poland, Czechoslovakia, Yugoslavia, Romania, Greece, Austria, Hungary, Bulgaria, Turkey, Finland, Albania, Lithuania, Latvia and Estonia [110: pp. 330–2].

But apart from stateless minorities such as the Jews, most self-declared champions of minority rights were motivated by an ill-disguised revisionist agenda. This applies above all to the defeated states that lost both territory and demographic substance: Germany, which lost Alsace-Lorraine, Poznania and Upper Silesia; Russia, which lost Congress Poland; and Hungary, which lost 70 per cent of its territory and 60 per cent of its population, mostly to Greater Romania [see statistical tables in the Appendix]. Weimar Germany under Foreign Minister Gustav Stresemann, for example, sought to prevent the loss of ethnic Germans living as minorities in the newly created states, particularly in Poland and Czechoslovakia. Stresemann clearly regarded it in Germany's interest as a revisionist power to support German minorities living outside the Weimar Republic's borders. This nationalist programme of supporting co-ethnics living outside the home territory enjoyed wide public support in the defeated states as such minorities were regarded as the living symbol and bridgeheads of revisionist claims. As Max Weber urged the German minorities in Poland and Czechoslovakia in December 1918: 'He, who in the threatened German irredenta is not prepared to employ revolutionary methods and to risk scaffold and prison, should not in future be called a *nationalist*' [84: p. 49; on German irredentism during the Weimar era, see also 110 and 64: pp. 112–34].

Nationalism was also the main cause for the rejection of demands to protect the rights of national and ethnic minorities. The big winners of the post-war settlement – particularly Poland and Romania – regarded such rights as a violation of their national sovereignty. They also considered them as a potentially destabilising force, a view that was shared by Great Britain, while France expected minorities to assimilate to the majority culture. What is decisive, however, and what determined the relationship between the three states we shall discuss in the following pages, is that all of them pursued a nationalist programme that rested on the following premises: that there existed an ethnonational core that had to be distinguished from the resident population (whether its members were citizens of the state or not) at large; that this ethnonational core legitimately owned the polity; that the state could not flourish as long as the ethnonational core did not predominate unambiguously in the cultural, linguistic, economic and political spheres of society; and that, where this predominance was indeed absent wholly or in part, specific action was needed to achieve it [this is based on 64: pp. 83–4]. The fateful dialectic between the nationalising policy of states like Poland and Romania on the one hand, and the homeland nationalism of revisionist states like Germany or Hungary on the other, created the kind of nationalist resentment that characterised the inter-war period [110: pp. 344–5; 102].

Poland

Poland provides an apt illustration of these dynamics. Recognised as a 'historic nation' that had long enjoyed Western sympathy, Poland's recreation at Versailles was supported by the Allies, not least because it was regarded as a 'Western bastion inhibiting German *revanche* and blocking Bolshevik expansion' [128: p. 161]. But the new Polish state was not a nation-state in the strict sense of the term: throughout the 1920s the Poles supplied no more than around 69 per cent of the total population, with Ukrainians, Jews, Germans, Lithuanians and Belorussians providing substantial minority populations [see maps and statistical table in the Appendix]. The Germans lived mainly in the western regions, while the Belorussians and Ukrainians were concentrated in the east. The Jews, although they lacked a clear regional concentration, played an important part in the urban economy. In terms of their occupational position, the Belorussians and Ukrainians were overwhelmingly agricultural, the Jews commercial and artisanal, while the Germans were mixed [129: pp. 35–8; 128: pp. 160–6].

Despite the existence of substantial minority populations living in post-war Poland, however, both officially and unofficially the new Polish state was conceived of as the state of and for the ethnolinguistically defined Polish nation. The 1921 constitution reflected this national vision. Not only were the minorities excluded from the constitution-drafting process but the constitution was also highly centralistic and insisted on the need for minorities to assimilate [129: p. 34]. To be sure, a glance at the political landscape of inter-war Poland reveals a variety of approaches and attitudes towards minorities. The political Right, which was allied with Roman Catholicism, was the staunchest proponent of an intolerant form of nationalism. It included the National Democrats, the Christian Democrats, and the National Labour Party, all of which were strong in ex-Prussian western Poland, and the Piast Peasant Party whose main constituency was the Polish peasantry of Galicia. For these groups, demands for national autonomy by minorities amounted to treason and justified a fierce response [129: p. 45; see also 122: p. 14]. The most militant form of Polish state nationalism manifested itself in the fierce conflict between the Polish authorities and Ukrainian nationalists in eastern Galicia. It also found expression in the rejection of Jewish calls for cultural autonomy and in a series of home-grown anti-Semitic policies, particularly in the 1930s. As Rothschild has demonstrated in his masterly political history of east central Europe, exceptions to this intolerant approach to the minority question included the Liberation Party, the Peasant Party, the Socialists and the Pilsudskist movement [129: pp. 31–45].

The so-called 'school strike' in Upper Silesia in 1926 demonstrates the degree of ethnic tension that the nation-building nationalism of the Polish state created. As indicated previously, Upper Silesia was a region in which Germans had formerly been predominant and the Poles subject to fierce (but largely unsuccessful) efforts at Germanisation by the Prussian state. After the war, the Polish educational authorities took measures designed to reduce the number of children attending minority schools as part of a programme of Polonisation. To this end, it conducted an enquiry among parents of children attending German minority schools. More than 8000 parents were interviewed. Based on the results, the authorities decided to disqualify 7114 children from attending such schools. This measure was taken after the parents of these children had either failed to take part in the official inquiry or because, when asked about the mother tongue of their children, they stated both Polish and German. This sparked a fierce response by German nationalists. The Deutscher Volksbund, which represented the Germans in Poland, protested to the League of Nations. In what amounts to a remarkable irony, given the Volksbund's commitment to a strictly ethnic conception of nationality, its representatives argued that membership in a national minority was a matter of personal choice. Yet the League of Nations supported the Polish point of view that nationality was objective rather than subjective, and that language was the ultimate criterion of legitimate nationhood. Polish-speaking children were expected to attend Polish rather than German minority schools. The Volksbund retaliated by sending a petition to the Council of the League. This led to a compromise which determined that children whose only language was Polish were not entitled to attend minority schools, while those who could prove a reasonable command of German (even if it was their second language) would be readmitted to minority schools [the incident is well documented in 110: pp. 341–2; 102].

From the Polish nationalist perspective, the German national minority in Poland constituted a 'fifth column' because their loyalty tended to rest with Germany, a revisionist power. Ethnic Germans were therefore increasingly perceived as unassimilable. From the mid-1920s onwards, the Polish policy therefore clearly revealed what Brubaker called 'dissimilationist' tendencies. In other words, rather than trying to assimilate the German minority, the Polish authorities pursued a strategy of more or less open exclusion. The measures adopted included the Polonisation of the civil service, the staging of anti-German demonstrations in the larger towns, the expropriation of German landlords, ethnic discrimination in business and the professions, and, increasingly, the implementation of strict mono-lingualism in public (including educational) institutions. Partly as a result of these measures, some two-thirds of the roughly 1.1 million ethnic Germans had left Poland by the mid-1920s, including 85 per cent of the urban population and 55 per cent of those employed in agriculture or related sectors [64: ch. 4]. Those who remained in the ex-Prussian provinces of Poland well into the 1930s despite these discriminatory policies – thereby fulfilling, as Max Weber and others had asked them to, the function of an irredentist frontier group – divided politically into Nazi supporters (the majority), bourgeois-nationalist, Catholic and socialist groups [129: pp. 41–2].

Romania

Although Romania's nationalist policies, not least in terms of the position taken towards minorities, was similar to that of Poland, Romania's historical legacy was quite different. Unlike the Polish lands, which had been divided among Prussia, Austria and Russia in the late eighteenth century, Romania had been an independent principality from 1878, becoming a kingdom in 1881. But this former Romanian kingdom, which joined the Allies in late 1916 in the hope of territorial gain, emerged as a massively enlarged state from the peace settlements. In terms of its total population and territorial expansion, Greater Romania, as the new entity came to be called, was more than twice the size of the old kingdom. With a population of around 18 million in 1930 (half of which lived in the pre-war Regate core, consisting of the principalities of Moldavia and Wallachia), Romania had become the second most populous state in east central Europe after Poland. It had acquired southern Dobrina (from Bulgaria), Bukovina (from Austria), Bessarabia (which had been under Russian rule since 1812), and Transylvania (part of historic Hungary). Ethnic Romanians constituted a clear majority of about 70 per cent of the total population. The three largest of the minority populations – Magyars, Germans and Jews – lived in the newly acquired provinces. In the Bukovina, for example, Ukrainians had formed a majority in 1910 (38.4 per cent), followed by Romanians (34.4 per cent), Jews (12 per cent) and Germans (9.3 per cent); and in the important province of Transylvania Magyars supplied a substantial ethnic contingent [see 119: p. 49; see statistical table in the Appendix].

However, in the official nationalist perspective the minority populations in the newly acquired territories – particularly Magyars and Jews – were perceived as 'foreigners' [129: pp. 281–8]. In this respect, the Magyars in Romania can be compared to the German minority in the newly created Poland. As a former ruling group retaining their loyalty to a revisionist state, the approximately 1.6 million-strong Magyar population acquired from 'Lesser Hungary' was seen as a constant threat to the stability of the Romanian nation-state. Like the Jews, they tended to be resented for the important role they played in the economy, the free professions and education in a country that even by eastern European standards was extremely backward. There were increasing doubts, certainly among leading Romanian nationalists, as to whether Magyars and Jews were assimilable. These resulted in the same dissimilationist tendencies that we observed for inter-war Poland, embodied in highly discriminatory measures that were officially labelled as assimilationist policies yet were designed, at least in part, to force particular groups to leave the state territory.

The Romanian authorities, like their Polish counterparts, subscribed to an ethnic brand of nationalism in which there was little, if any, room for the cultural aspirations of minorities. This attitude was further reinforced as a result of the massive territorial enlargement and concomitant acquisition of substantial minority populations that followed the First World War. As in Poland, albeit even more pronounced, the nationalising project of the Romanian authorities was particularly manifest in the educational sector. As Irina Livezeanu has demonstrated in her account of Romanian cultural politics, the National Liberal government in particular embarked on a massive programme of educational reform. This programme was officially described as a 'cultural offensive' by its protagonist, Constantin Angelescu [119: p. 35]. Romanian official nationalism, which had its strongholds in the old kingdom with its French-educated bureaucratic elite and in Transylvania, regarded the minorities' efforts to maintain their culture and identity as a threat to the prosperity and integrity of the Romanian nation.

The number of primary schools more than doubled between 1918 and the end of the 1930s, as did the number of teachers; a network of committees was established at the local level, while the school system was standardised through the creation of 16 school districts. In terms of educational content, there was an increased emphasis on the teaching of the Romanian language, Romanian history, geography and civics, and the remaining non-Romanian schools were required to adopt this new curriculum. Although Romania's official, secular nationalism was also directed against the strong regional identities of ethnic Romanians – most obviously in Transylvania, where the Orthodox and Uniate churches continued to provide an alternative source of collective identity to the secular state – its main preoccupation was the Romanisation of minority cultures. In the Bukovina, for example, Greater Romania's smallest province in the north and formerly part of the Austrian state, the number of Romanian schools increased dramatically at the expense of Ukrainian and German ones. The Romanian authorities, in an attempt to circumvent the Minority Protection Treaty they had been forced to sign by the Allies, argued that the Ukrainians were 'Ruthenized Romanians who needed to be returned to their free Romanian identity' [119: p. 65].

The resistance that these attitudes and related policies provoked among the minorities only served to harden the stance of many policy makers and officials, leading to a vicious circle of tension and conflict. As a 1923 government report described the situation in Bukovina, a province that the Romanian nation-builders tried to cleanse of its Austrian cultural legacy:

> The teachers from Region No. XIV, almost all of them raised in submission to the Austrian state, have started to realize that the Romanian state has a durability that no one can overturn. They have started to reconcile themselves to the idea of a Romanian state and they bow before the authority of this state the more decisive the measures which the government takes vis-à-vis any citizen in order to defend the prestige of this state and to remind everyone that one has obligations toward the state which one cannot evade. [cited in 119: p. 78]

In the former Russian province of Bessarabia, too, the Romanian authorities embarked on a cultural project of Romanisation. In the mid-1930s they began to sound the alarm bells after several school inspectors had detected reluctance among Ukrainians, Russians and Jews to learn the Romanian language [119: pp. 117–20].

Transylvania presents a particularly interesting example because its ethnic Romanian population – hardened in its nationalist resolve in the long struggle against Magyarisation that had only come to an end with Hungary's defeat in the war – actively participated in the state's cultural policy of Romanisation. From the ethnonationalist point of view adhered to by the Romanian authorities, the demographic situation in Transylvania was highly critical. In 1910, the total population of Transylvania was 5,263,602. Of those, 53.8 per cent were ethnic Romanians, 31.6 per cent Hungarians, 10.7 per cent Germans, and 3.5 per cent Jews [119: p. 135]. The dominant cultural influences in Transylvania prior to the war had been Hungarian and German, with the Jews showing a clear preference for adopting the linguistic culture of either one of these two privileged groups. A mass exodus of some 197,000 Magyars to Hungary (i.e. about one-fifth of Transylvania's Magyar population) after the Treaty of Trianon had been signed in June 1920 only served to increase the suspicion among Romanian nationalists that the Hungarians posed a potential threat to the Romanian state. The western border of Transylvania with Hungary thus witnessed one of the fiercest programmes of Romanian cultural nationalism. As Livezeanu notes in her excellent book on this subject: 'In the west, Romanization was applied more harshly, in keeping with the memory of Hungarians as an overbearing elite and with the fear of Hungarian revisionism' [119: p. 143].

Hence the pattern of nationalist conflict we encounter in Transylvania, played out between Romanian nationalists and a Magyar minority mostly loyal to the Hungarian state, is similar to that of the conflict between the Polish authorities and the German minority in the former Prussian provinces. In effect, then, the nationalist struggle in these regions led to a self-fulfilling prophecy insofar as each side saw their own prejudices confirmed by the actions of the other side. The Magyars in Transylvania and the Germans in Poland's western provinces showed all the hallmarks of a frontier nationality, an attitude that was encouraged, where encouragement was needed, by the irredentism of a revisionist power. From the point of view of the exponents of the Polish and Romanian states, the attitude and actions of these minorities posed a severe threat that invited a cultural counter-offensive. Yet the constant pressure exerted by the Romanian and Polish states on these national minorities only served to reinforce the nationalist resolve of the Transylvanian Hungarians and the Germans in Poland respectively. They were locked in a vicious nationalist circle.

Czechoslovakia

One state that emerged from the post-war settlement contrasts in many respects rather markedly with the rest of eastern Europe, including both Poland and Romania. That state is Czechoslovakia. To begin with, Czechoslovakia was the most obviously manufactured of the 'successor' states besides Yugoslavia. The political union between Czechs and Slovaks, which formed the core of the new state, was the product of the tireless diplomacy of the politicians Tomaš Masaryk and Edvard Beneš. Czechoslovakia's relative political stability was the result of strong presidential powers (and the strong leadership of T. Masaryk) and a coalition system that provided opportunities for all major parties. From 1926 onwards, for example, the Sudeten Germans, no loyal supporters of the Czechoslovak state, formed part of the government [136: p. 218].

Besides being the only functioning democracy in eastern Europe between the wars, Czechoslovakia was also the most industrialised and urbanised region of eastern Europe. The percentage of the population employed in the agricultural, industrial and commercial sectors was respectively 39.5, 33.8 and 5.78 in 1921, and 34.6, 34.9 and 7.43 in 1930. Of course, there was considerable regional variation. Bohemia was Czechoslovakia's most advanced region in economic terms, followed by Moravia-Silesia, while Slovakia (whose population had been subjected to Hungarian rule and its Magyarisation policies since 1867) and Ruthenia remained heavily agricultural during the entire period (the figures are approximately 60 per cent for Slovakia and 66 per cent for Ruthenia). While illiteracy levels in Bohemia, Moravia and Silesia decreased from around 3 to below 2 per cent between 1921 and 1930, they were higher in Slovakia (from 14.7 per cent to 8.16 per cent) and Ruthenia (50.03 to 30.88 per cent). These disparities in economic and cultural development are also manifest in the degree of urbanisation within the individual provinces [see 129: pp. 91–2, 117–18; 136: pp.171–2].

However, like the other major beneficiaries of the peace settlements, Czechoslovakia was ethnically diverse, which caused problems both domestically and with respect to foreign relations. The inclusion of substantial national minorities living along its borders – over 3 million

Germans in the Sudetenland, 2.5 million Slovaks (although the Slovaks were not recognised as a minority in official censuses), 700,000 Hungarians in the south of Slovakia, 75,000 Poles in the economically important and fiercely contested region of Cieszyn in Silesia – meant that most of its neighbours harboured irredentist claims against Czechoslovakia from the moment its independence was proclaimed on 28 November 1918. Throughout the inter-war period, relations with Hungary, Poland and Germany remained marked by deep distrust and open hostility [129: pp. 78, 85–7; 107: pp. 132–4; for population statistics see Appendix].

Although the government's official stance towards the aspirations of national minorities was not as repressive as that of its neighbours, the Czechs dominated the new state both politically and culturally. Czechoslovak nationality policy, although comparatively liberal on paper, was more ambivalent and contentious in practice. The roughly 2.5 million Slovaks (constituting 16 per cent of the total population), for example, were expected to adopt the cultural norms and values of the around 7.25 million Czechs, who made up 48 per cent of the total population. The 'Pittsburgh Agreement' (signed in May 1918 between Masaryk and Slovak *émigrés* in the United States), in which the Slovaks had been guaranteed autonomy within a future Czecho-Slovak state, was never implemented. In fact, the authorities' refusal to recognise Slovak autonomy within the newly created state of Czechoslovakia (from 1920 onwards the hyphen was dropped in official usage) was a deliberate strategy to downplay the fact that Czechs did not constitute a majority within the state. Czech officials had a strong presence in Slovakia, regarding themselves as colonisers of a backward region. Rather than assimilating Slovaks to dominant Czech culture, these measures provoked resentment among the local population and strengthened Slovak nationalism, which by the 1930s had become a recognisable force [see 128: pp. 149–54; see also statistical tables in the Appendix].

But the fiercest of all inter-ethnic conflicts in inter-war Czechoslovakia, and the one which came to pose a serious threat to the state's stability, was that between the Czechs and the Sudeten Germans. At the Paris peace negotiations, the Czechoslovak Foreign Minister Beneš declared his government's intention to create the Czechoslovak state on the Swiss consociational model, provided such a solution was commensurate with the conditions in the Czech and Slovak lands. In his speech before the National Assembly in Prague in December 1918, however, Masaryk chose a different tone. In this much-noticed address, he reminded the Sudeten Germans that they had once come as immigrants and colonists. He then added that the new government would not allow them to challenge Czechoslovakia's territorial integrity. Masaryk's statement must be placed in the context of the events that accompanied the declaration of Czechoslovak independence. After the republic had been proclaimed on 28 November 1918, the Sudeten Germans refused to accept its jurisdictional authority by declaring Deutschböhmen and the Sudetenland as independent provinces of Austria. When it became clear that neither Austria nor Germany was in a position to lend active support to these claims, the Czech Legion troops occupied these regions in December [129: p. 79; 128: pp. 151–3].

Public symbols became a focal point in the nationality conflict between Czechs and Sudeten Germans. The so-called statues war of the 1920s provides a particularly illuminating example of how nationalism triggered a struggle over the symbolic representation of the past. In the course of this conflict, statues of Joseph II were attacked and toppled by Czechs. The late eighteenth-century Kaiser Joseph II, a proponent of administrative centralisation, had antagonised many Czechs (as well as other Slavs and the Magyars) by declaring German the lingua franca of the monarchy. For the German nationalists in the Bohemian lands, meanwhile, Joseph II stood for past glory and German predominance in Bohemia. The monuments to Joseph II had begun to spring up thick and fast during the 1880s, during the period, that is, when Bohemia was experiencing a Czech national revival aided by rapid industrialisation, emigration and urbanisation. The fact that Joseph II was no nationalist – his decision to declare German the language of imperial administration was inspired by his programme of enlightened absolutism – mattered little to the Czechs. For them, Joseph II stood for the promotion of German ethnic dominance in Bohemia. The fact that the German minority in Bohemia openly praised Joseph II as a champion of the German cause in the Czech lands seemed to confirm this perception. As Wingfield observes in her stimulating article: 'German nationalists thus appropriated the memory of Joseph II and interpreted his actions for their own ends, claiming the *Volkskaiser* as the emperor of the German *Volk*' [139: p. 153]. Czech intellectuals were ambivalent in their judgement of Joseph II's legacy. They acknowledged his educational reforms and were highly sympathetic to his achievements in such matters as religious tolerance and the abolition of serfdom. But they tended to resent him for his centralising and Germanising policies, which in their view had threatened their language and culture [139: p. 162].

71

The recorded attacks on monuments of Joseph II in northern and western Bohemia, most of which took place in 1919 and 1920, were not encouraged by the Czech authorities, though there is evidence that local officials remained remarkably passive [139: p. 150]. Most of these incidents took place on or around 28 October, when Czechs celebrated their national independence. A particularly notorious incident occurred in Brno in the summer of 1919. After a Czech crowd had knocked down statues of Joseph II, German nationalists responded by singing the nationalist song 'Die Wacht am Rhein'. Another notable event was reported from the town of Eger, where a statue had been knocked from its pedestal, only to be erected again by the German inhabitants, who then proceeded to drape the statue in black, red and gold. Some German demonstrators then headed for the town's recently opened Czech-language school, causing damage to the furniture and tearing up pictures of President Masaryk. This particular incident triggered off a nation-wide protest, organised by the Northern Bohemian National Union, a national pressure group founded in 1885 to defend Czech interests in the German-dominated border regions of Bohemia. In all these instances, seemingly small symbolic provocations sufficed to spark a major nationalist conflict [139: pp. 150–1].

The Jewish minority and the emergence of Zionism

The previous explorations have examined the effects of nation-building nationalism on national minorities. Yet ethnic minorities such as the Ukrainians, Lithuanians, Belorussians, Sinti and Roma, or Jews were equally affected by the nationalist policies of states like Poland, Romania or Czechoslovakia. Unlike national minorities such as the Germans in Poland or the Hungarians in Romania, they could not migrate to a state where they constituted the majority. The situation of ethnic minorities, to cite Michael Hechter, was characterised by a 'limitation on exit' [114: p. 31]. It is in this context that nationalism provided an inspiration and a potential way out of the quandary of being a state-less minority in a Europe whose states subscribed to a nationalist agenda. Such nationalist ambitions could take either of two basic forms. The first consisted of a programme for cultural autonomy within a given state. The second found expression in calls for political self-determination. Ethnic minorities, including the Ukrainians, the Latvians and the Jews, had begun to develop such ambitions in the late nineteenth century, but it was not until the inter-war period that calls for cultural autonomy and/or for independent statehood gained wide currency among these groups.

The Zionist movement, which was officially founded at the First Zionist Congress in Basel in 1898, proposed a nationalist solution to the predicament of the Jews in central and eastern Europe. While a considerable literature has sprung up dealing with this manifestation of Jewish nationalism, the phenomenon has received rather little attention in general accounts of nationalism. This is surprising not just because Zionism cannot be understood outside the context of European nationalism, but also because few nationalist movements offer a better insight into the dynamics of inter-war nationalism and its effects on minority populations [on this see 133: p. xvii; 134: p. 363].

In more than one sense, Zionism was a product of European nationalism. For one thing, Zionists drew positive inspiration from the classic nationalist demands – expressed above all in the concept of national self-determination, but also in the claim to independent statehood. For another, Zionism was a response to anti-Semitic discrimination, violence and persecution, which was an integral part of inter-war nationalism in central and eastern Europe. Apart from these specific and largely contingent circumstances, Zionism also benefited from a cultural legacy that could easily be translated into a modern nationalist idiom. Of particular importance was the concept of a shared homeland. The memory of an ancient Jewish kingdom, and of the expulsion of the Jewish people from Palestine, was a firm part of Jewish religious and historical legacy. Although religious scriptures and institutions played a decisive part in the preservation of this memory over several centuries, it was not confined to religiously observant Jews. This teleological vision of restoring the ancient state, while it did not create Jewish nationalism, provided fertile ground for Zionist agitators to develop a secular narrative in line with modern nationalist demands [see, for example, 132: p. 448].

The predicament of an ethnic minority in a context of nationalism

What sets Zionism apart from other nationalist movements is that historically Europe's Jews lacked both a single territorial affiliation and thus a legitimate claim to national homeland on the continent. Although Jewish communities were particularly numerous in the east, European Jewry had never been concentrated in a single territory but lived geographically dispersed over the whole continent. Broadly speaking, Zionism can thus be defined as an attempt to solve the 'Jewish question' (a term used prominently by Theodor Herzl and other Zionist leaders) not through assimilation but through the creation of a Jewish state outside Europe [134: pp. 4-5; on important Zionist intellectuals, see 133; for a critical assessment of the historiography on Zionism, see 105].

The largest number of Jews in non-communist Europe lived in Poland. (More than 6 million, constituting by far the largest Jewish community anywhere between the wars, resided in Soviet Russia.) The approximately 3.1 million Jews residing in Poland in 1931 constituted about 9.8 per cent of the total population. The corresponding figures in 1930 for Romania, the country with the second largest Jewish community in east central Europe, are approximately 756,000 and 4.2 per cent. The 1930 census for Czechoslovakia, the third state we have considered in some detail, showed a total Jewish population of 356,830, representing 2.42 per cent of the total population. By comparison, the proportion of Jews in Germany's total population in 1910 was just 0.95 per cent, and it was considerably lower in France. This was considerably less than in post-Trianon Hungary, where in 1920 there were 473,355 Jews constituting 5.9 per cent of the state population [122: pp. 99–102, 142–4, 178–83; 61: p. 313].

In all the states of east central Europe with substantial Jewish populations, Jews represented the most urbanised group. The percentage of Jews against the total urban population tended to be highest in the more backward regions. In Poland, for example, Jews constituted about 30 per cent of the total urban population, and in the eastern parts of Poland such as Galicia it was over 50 per cent. In Romania, the highest urban concentration of Jews was in Bessarabia and Bukovina, where in some cities it was between 30 and 40 per cent. In the largest cities of Poland, Romania and Czechoslovakia the proportion of Jews among the total population after the First World War was as follows: Kracow (33.4 per cent), Bucharest (11.8 per cent), Prague (4.17 per cent). Jews were also over-represented in the industrial and commercial sectors of the economy. In Poland in 1921, 34 per cent of the Jewish population were occupied in industry and mines, while 41.3 per cent worked in commerce and insurance, and 5.8 per cent earned their living in the agricultural sector. In Romania in 1930, the percentage of the Jewish population in the economy was as follows: commerce and credit (48.3), industry and craft (32.8), agriculture

(4.1), civil service and professions (21.7) [122: pp. 23–31, 142–4, 178–83].

National cultural autonomy or territorial nationalism?

Zionism represents an extremely complex and differentiated phenomenon, and the term 'movement' should therefore not be used to imply a high degree of convergence in terms of either doctrine or method. To the outside observer, its history often appears like a struggle between different ideological currents sharing a common aim but disagreeing profoundly on the means to be adopted to accomplish it. The contours of Zionism may become clearer when considered against the broader context of Jewish responses to modern nationalism in Europe. Following an article by Henry Tobias [123: pp. 101–21], we can distinguish three broad approaches. The first, which had its proponents especially among sections of the Jewish bourgeoisie and the radical Left, regarded assimilation as the most appropriate strategy to resolve the Jewish question. This was the view favoured by Theodor Herzl only a few years before the publication of *The Jewish State: An Attempt at a Modern Solution to the Jewish Question* in 1896 [116: p. 33]. Part of the Jewish Enlightenment movement (Haskalah), which was particularly strong in eastern Galicia and Russia, advocated partial assimilation as a solution to the problems the Jews were facing in these societies.

In Congress Poland, the members of the affluent Jewish commercial class were highly assimilated to Polish culture by the end of the nineteenth century [122: pp. 19–20]. But attitudes to Jewish assimilation varied widely among the Polish majority. In inter-war Poland, for example, some, particularly on the Left, actively encouraged the Jews to assimilate into Polish culture because they did not see the Jews as a nation. Further to the right of the political spectrum we find those who opposed Jewish assimilation because they thought Jews could not be assimilated. For radical nationalists like Dmowski and his disciples, the aim was to rid Poland of its Jewish population [122: p. 38].

Flowing from the emancipatory traditions of the Jewish socialist movement and from a cultural nationalism that had been among the ascendancy among eastern Europe's ethnic and national groups since the late nineteenth century, a second, and on the whole more influential, approach saw the solution to the 'Jewish question' in the granting of national cultural autonomy by those states with large Jewish populations. Those who subscribed to it assumed that the Jews formed a distinctive people or nation whose cultural legacy was worth preserving. To achieve this aim of cultural self-preservation they proposed *Gegenwartsarbeit* – activities designed to strengthen the cultural and political position of the Jewish communities in the various European states. But unlike the political Zionists, the proponents of this approach did not link the concept of cultural autonomy to political demands for independent statehood. In 1892, K. Liberman, the founder of the socialist *arbeter fraynd* ('Worker's Friend', a newspaper founded in London's East End in 1891 by Jewish immigrants from eastern Europe), gave a remarkable account of this attempt to fuse a Jewish national revival with socialist internationalism: 'We have to be Jewish, and on no account be ashamed of that. We have to be somewhat national; to be Jewish patriots a bit. Of course, such patriotism must not be exaggerated. We cannot be Palestinian patriots. We should unite with all the socialists who advocate internationalist ideas, and yet we should still remain national (not nationalistic)' [cited in Frankel in 123: p. 74; on *Gegenwartsarbeit* see also 134: pp. 10–11].

The concept of national cultural autonomy also found some support within the most important socialist Jewish organisation in eastern Europe, the Bund (founded in Vilna in 1897). Yet the concept remained highly contested. Thus at the Bund's Fourth Congress in 1902, the delegates showed considerable support for the view that nationality was a legitimate concept, and that different nations could be distinguished on the basis of language, customs, way of life and culture in general. Yet the proposal that the Jews should strive for national cultural autonomy, proposed at the Fifth Congress in Zürich in June 1903, narrowly failed [Tobias in 123: pp. 112–16]. Between the wars, however, the Bund became more favourable to the concept of national cultural autonomy. At the same time, and in spite of rising violence against Jews, it remained adamantly opposed to Zionism's territorial nationalism. As one of its leaders, Vladimir Medem, declared in 1920: 'We are asked why we are opposed to Zionism. The answer is simple: because we are socialists. And not merely socialistically inclined or socialists in name only, but active socialists. And between Zionist activity and Socialist activity there is a fundamental and profound chasm. . .. Across that chasm there is no bridge' [cited in Polonsky in 123: p. 172; see also Jacobs in 123: p. 505].

In contrast to the champions of cultural autonomy, political Zionists advocated a territorial brand of nationalism that aimed at establishing a Jewish state in Palestine. But even within political Zionism there was fierce disagreement on which strategy and timetable one ought to follow. Those following the legacy of Theodor Herzl emphasised the need for diplomatic negotiation with the main powers before large-scale emigration to Palestine could occur. Others, like Vladimir Jabotinsky and his supporters in Russia, favoured a more activist and militantly nationalist approach that focused on migration and colonisation [133: p. 208; on the Russian Zionists around Jabotinsky and Trumpeldor, see 134: pp. 137–42]. Yet at their annual conference in 1917, the Russian Zionists supported a programme that defined a Jewish national homeland in Palestine as 'the ultimate long-term aim'; this was combined with the demand for 'equal national rights for the Jews in Russia itself' and calls for 'loyal Jewish participation in the movement for a democratic, secular, multinational Russian state'. There can be little doubt that the creation of new states in east central Europe in the aftermath of the First World War added legitimacy to the doctrines and aims of the political Zionists [134: pp. 257, 28–30; 122: pp. 57–8].

Determinants of Jewish nationalism

What contributed most directly to Zionism's increasing appeal, besides the view that nationalism provided a solution to the Jewish predicament, were the anti-Semitic policies that several states introduced during the inter-war period. In Poland and Romania in particular, Jews suffered discrimination from both official and unofficial sources. Both states had granted Jews formal civil emancipation under pressure, and both revoked it within a matter of years. In ex-Austrian Galicia, for example, Jews ceased to play a role in the civil service when the Polish state was established after the war. Discriminatory measures were also directed against Jews occupied in the free professions, and there were hardly any Jews employed in higher education. By the late 1930s these measures had led to the economic impoverishment of Jews in Poland. At least as far as the Jews were concerned, the nationality policies of Poland became more or less openly dissimilationist in the course of the 1930s [122: p. 42; 134: p. 358].

The same can be said of Romania. Here, too, Jews were strongly represented in the urban economy, but remained largely excluded from the civil service, law and the teaching profession. Given that Romanian nationalists glorified rural life and elevated the Romanian peasant to a symbol of pure and authentic nationhood, Jews appeared as the natural outsiders and as the preferred objects of stigmatisation. In an attempt to keep Jewish numbers down, from the 1890s onwards Jews were forced to pay tuition fees in Romanian state secondary schools. Throughout the inter-war years, moreover, both Polish and Romanian universities, in which Jewish students had been traditionally over-represented, remained hotbeds of anti-Semitic agitation [119: pp. 197–9; 122: pp. 73–4; on anti-Semitism in inter-war Austria, see 116: pp. 56–61].

But it was not just active exclusion as a result of discriminatory measures that the Jews of central and eastern Europe faced from the 1890s. Even before the outbreak of the war, eastern Europe had witnessed a number of pogroms (and consequently Jewish emigration to central and western European countries). Such incidents proliferated and intensified during the inter-war period. Especially in the immediate aftermath of the First World War, with many border disputes and national conflicts still unresolved, pogroms occurred in several countries. The worst such incidents took place in ethnically mixed areas where the aspirations of the new state-nation clashed with those of another nationality who sought independence for itself. Eastern Galicia and Lithuania were particularly affected. Both Polish lands had come under occupation during the war, exposing the Jews to nationalist accusations of collaboration. When a fierce conflict erupted in eastern Galicia between the Poles and Ukrainians at the end of the war – a Ukrainian Republic was declared in the autumn of 1918 – both Poles and Ukrainians accused the Jews of supporting their enemy. The fact that the local Jewish National Council had proclaimed neutrality in the conflict made little difference, as the vicious pogrom in Lemberg in November 1918, and the various outbursts of violence against Jews in the subsequent months, made glaringly obvious [122: pp. 40–52; 113: pp. 8–13; 134: p. 359].

The rise of authoritarian regimes and political parties during the 1930s exacerbated the situation even further. The increasingly radical nature of Polish domestic politics during the 1930s went hand in hand with an upsurge of anti-Jewish violence. Pogroms occurred in Grodno in 1935, in Prztyk and Minsk-Mazowiecki in 1936, and in Brzesc in 1937 [122: p. 74]. A 1937 government report, while condemning attacks against Jews, justified economic discrimination as a means to defend Polish culture from Jewish influence. As early as 1935, the Peasant Party had declared that the Jews could not be assimilated to Polish ways. The manifesto concluded with an open declaration of support for the Zionist programme [122: p. 72].

Young Jews especially who had been brought up in relatively assimilated families began to express deep frustration, even disillusionment, at the lack of prospects in Poland. As one Jewish youth wrote in 1930: 'If one were to ask me to give a simple definition of the period in which we live, I would answer: a hopeless generation' [cited in 122: p. 76]. Another, also writing in the 1930s, retrospectively attributed the attraction Zionism exerted on him to the bleak prospects for his generation in a social environment in which open discrimination went hand in hand with a rhetoric of equal rights:

> At home here there was no prospect for the future. Business was bad. I did not see any prospects for a future after I finished school. And at home I was being threatened with an interruption of school. And even in this tragic situation, despite no prospects for the future, I wanted to finish school . . . If anyone would ask me then what I would do after finishing school, I would not have known the answer. In this terrible situation I took to Zionism like a drowning person to a board. [cited in 122: p. 78]

Yet as mentioned previously, Zionism was not just the product of virulent anti-Semitism. The Zionists also drew positive inspiration from nationalism as a movement that within the space of a few decades had altered much of Europe's geographical and political landscape. To some extent this had already been the case before the war. The Jews in Prussia, for example, witnessed Polish national aspirations at first hand in the late nineteenth century. The Ukrainian nationalist movement, although it was crushed by the Polish state, also exerted a powerful influence on the Jews of eastern Galicia. But it was the triumph of the principle of national self-determination after the First World War that dramatically increased Zionism's appeal among the Jewish masses [134: p. 222]. At the same time, the fact that the majority of the newly created states did not tolerate Jewish aspirations for cultural autonomy tended to vindicate the Zionist argument that the future of the Jews lay outside Europe.

This chapter has focused on the impact of state-building nationalism on minorities. It was emphasised that in the so-called successor states the Wilsonian principle of national self-determination was interpreted as the right of the dominant nationality to impose its culture on the minority populations living within a particular state territory. The gravest threat to the principles of democracy and cultural pluralism would emanate not from nationalism, however, but from the rise of fascism from the late 1920s onwards. This is the theme that will concern us in the next chapter.

4 Homeland Nationalism Gone Wild: Nationalism and Fascism

Although fascist-style movements advocating race hatred continue to make headlines in twenty-first-century Europe, few would argue that fascism still poses an imminent threat to European democracy. The picture was different in the 1930s when, in Eric Hobsbawm's words, fascism 'looked like the wave of the future' [150: p. 112]. While fascism is a highly complex phenomenon that cannot be attributed to a single cause, it is worth exploring its relation to nationalism. How important was nationalism for the rise of fascism as an ideology and political movement? Was fascism simply nationalism turned radical, as a majority of historians seem to believe? Or are we to follow the advice of those scholars who argue that we should treat nationalism and fascism as two separate historical phenomena? Most of the pertinent literature addresses the pivotal question of the relationship between nationalism and fascism implicitly and *en passant* rather than systematically [as we shall see further below, the two exceptions are 28 and 163].

The first part of this chapter outlines the state of the scholarly debate on fascism in terms of its main approaches and theoretical positions. The second part stresses the affinity between organic and irredentist forms of nationalism and fascist movements. In these kinds of nationalism 'the nation' is seen as an organic whole whose integrity is actually or potentially threatened by 'foreign elements' within or (in the case of national minorities living outside their homeland state) by the assimilationist policies of a 'foreign state'. The focus of this chapter will therefore be on the potential significance of these forms of nationalism for mobilising mass support for fascist movements. It goes without saying that fascist mass mobilisation needs to be related to many other factors – particularly to the crisis in economic and political conditions after the First World War – which have little if anything to do with nationalism.

There is therefore no suggestion, not even implictly, that nationalism holds the key to any understanding of fascism. What also needs to be stressed is that I shall not examine fascism at regime level. Both nationalism and fascism will be treated as ideological and political movements. When exploring the links between the two, the focus will thus be on affinities in terms of doctrines, political strategies and aims.

Rival interpretations of fascism

The complexity of fascism as a modern historical phenomenon is reflected in persistent disagreement and controversy regarding its nature and, above all, its causes. Reductionist theories of fascism that centre on class warfare or certain psychological dispositions have generally been discarded in favour of more nuanced historical accounts that concentrate on several factors and their mutual interaction. There is now less interest, it seems, in general theories of fascism than in concepts and approaches that may help elucidate certain of its manifestations. There are different definitions of fascism, but the following three elements seem to figure in most of them: an ultranationalism that emphasises the need for an organic rebirth of society; mass mobilisation around a charismatic leader; and, finally, the justification of violence not just as a political means but its glorification as an end in itself [see, for example, 161: p. 14]. The heart of the current controversy concerns the question of whether fascism is best explained by reference to cultural and ideological traditions, domestic politics and institutional breakdowns, geopolitical challenges, or economic crises [on the conceptual debate, see 147: chs. 1 and 2 and 149; for a comprehensive survey of both the history and historiography of fascism, see 161].

The existence of different interpretations notwithstanding, two things are uncontested among students of fascism. The first concerns the crucial significance of the First World War. Scholars are in agreement that the war itself, and particularly its outcome, was conducive to the proliferation of fascist movements across Europe. Without the severe political crisis of the inter-war period, so the general consensus goes, it is unlikely that the fascists would have crossed the threshold of power in Germany and Italy and enjoyed considerable successes in Romania, Hungary and a few other cases [see, for example, Eley in 140; 161: pp. 71–9; 150: 126–7]. Not only did the First World War produce the kind of institutional instability on which political extremism of various kinds could grow – particularly in the societies of the defeated states – but the war itself was also the formative experience in the lives of many who would later join fascist organisations, or even played a dominant part in their creation: 19 per cent of fascist leaders in inter-war Europe had a military career background; many, including Hitler, had served at the front [156: p. 55; on the role of the front soldier in fascist mythology and politics, see, for example, 86].

The second point of convergence is more pertinent to the theme of this book. There is wide agreement that nationalism played a huge part in the emergence of fascism as an ideology and a movement. As Juan J. Linz wrote in an extensive and influential article on the social composition of fascist movements and their followers:

> Fascism is above all a nationalist movement and therefore wherever the nation and the state are strongly identified it also exalts the authority of the state, and its supremacy over all social groups and conflicting interests. . . . For complex historical reasons, nationalism occupied a very different place in the minds of people in different societies and this probably accounts for the relative strength of fascism more than any other variable. [156: p. 15]

Geoff Eley, too, links fascism to the emergence of 'radical nationalism' in the decades before the First World War [142: p. 266], while Eugen Weber notes fascists' violent obsession with national unity [98: p. 274]. Other leading scholars of fascism, including George L. Mosse, Stanley Payne, Zeev Sternhell and Roger Griffin, have been equally keen to stress the part played by nationalism in the formation of fascist movements. Roger Griffin has identified 'a palingenetic form of populist ultra-nationalism' as the one feature that was common to all fascist movements. This kind of nationalism is composed of three building blocks: a myth of revival or rebirth that emphasises the need for communal (political, economic or cultural) regeneration; a direct appeal to 'the people' (rather than to an elected parliament) as the source of political legitimacy; the view that the nation forms a natural community whose members owe it (and the charismatic leader figure who incarnates its spirit) their absolute loyalty [147: pp. 32–7]. Finally, Mosse has described nationalism as a 'belief-system which provided the foundation for all fascist movements, it was the bed rock upon which they were built' [158: p. xi; 161: p. 14].

Yet in spite of the apparent scholarly consensus about the significance of nationalism for fascism in Europe, the specific connections between the two phenomena are still much less clear than might be expected. In part this is because what has commonly been termed 'radical nationalism' has often been more or less equated with fascism. The assumption is that if nationalism becomes extreme – 'radical', 'tribal' and 'palingenetic' are just some of the adjectives used in this context – it will almost inevitably turn into (or at least become indistinguishable from) fascism. There is no doubt that nationalism and fascism were closely related in practice. However, I shall argue that this can best be seen if the two phenomena are kept separate for analytical purposes. Thus rather than assuming that the latter evolved automatically from the former, I shall ask which type of nationalist argument was woven into the fabric of fascist ideology, and under what conditions such arguments were used by fascist movements in order to mobilise mass support.

The main issue that tends to divide students of fascism, including the two scholars of nationalism (John Breuilly and Anthony D. Smith) who have explicitly engaged with the phenomenon, concerns the impact of ideological and cultural factors on the formation of fascist movements. Whereas scholars such as George W. Mosse, Stanley Payne, Zeev Sternhell and Roger Griffin have insisted that such factors are indeed essential, others, including Robert O. Paxton, John Breuilly and Geoff Eley, have concentrated on politics and on the context in which fascist movements take shape.

Culture, ideology and continuity

The cultural interpretation of fascism has been pioneered by George L. Mosse and subsequently been elaborated in the works of Stanley Payne, Zeev Sternhell and Roger Griffin, to name but the most prominent exponents of this approach. Mosse has repeatedly argued that the study of fascism should not be restricted to an examination of the social composition of its protagonists and followers or of the economic-cum-political crisis that shattered central and eastern Europe in the wake of the First World War [see 157; 87; 158]. While conceding the importance of objective factors in explaining fascist successes, he nevertheless stresses the importance of public perception and symbolism. For Mosse, a large part of fascism's popular appeal derived from its ability to provide a source of meaning and orientation in a world marked by uncertainties and status anxieties. Fascism was experienced as status-enhancing by those suffering from the syndrome that sociologists have termed *anomie,* manifested in status loss, disappointed expectations, and profound uncertainty about future developments. 'In times of crisis', Mosse argues, fascist programmes 'provided many millions of people with a more meaningful involvement than representative parliamentary government. This is why fascism's appeal must be primarily sought in the specific content of the language and rhetoric fostered by its leaders and their organisations.' 'Political choices', to quote Mosse again, 'are determined by people's actual perception of their situation, their hopes and longings, the utopia toward which they strive' [158: p. 44]. Crucially, fascists used cultural idioms and symbols that were familiar and thus resonated with the public: romanticism, nationalism, notions of direct democracy and organic communalism, millenarianism, religious ritual and imagery, masculine aestheticism, racism, the veneration of youth – all these values had gained currency in the course of the nineteenth century.

For Mosse, the specific significance of nationalism for fascism derives in part from its ability to fuse several of these existing values into an apparently coherent ideological blend or *Weltanschauung*, as well as its supplying the fascists with a familiar liturgy and civil religion whose origins go back to the festivals of the French Revolution. The concept of the general will, of national regeneration, of authenticity, ideas about nature and organic growth, and the populist vision of a class-less community or *Volk* could all form part of the nationalist synthesis. From the late nineteenth century, and particularly in Germany, France and eastern Europe, social Darwinist fantasies about superiority and inferiority, about human existence as a struggle for survival, as well as anti-Semitic visions about the degenerating influence of Jews, were added to the canon [157: pp. 41–59]. Through the experience of the First World War, they were reactivated and radicalised. Concepts such as youth and masculinity became brutalised as they were amalgamated into a new revolutionary ideology that promised the resurrection of the fatherland and its liberation from the humiliation of defeat and the philistine restrictions of bourgeois life. Thus although Mosse implicitly distinguishes between nationalism and fascism, he nevertheless insists on the close affinity between many right-wing nationalisms and fascism, racism and anti-Semitism. As he notes: 'Nationalism imagining itself under siege tended to become racist, projecting a counter-type and, like that of the Jews, locking it into place as the external enemy' [13: p. 170].

Another eminent exponent of a culturalist approach to fascism is Zeev Sternhell, who locates the roots of inter-war fascism in *fin-de-siècle* intellectual developments. For Sternhell, the First World War, rather than producing fascism, radicalised currents of thought that had been taking shape in the last third of the nineteenth century. Among the thinkers who contributed to the emergence of a proto-fascist idiom Sternhell singles out the Italians d'Annunzio and Corradini, the Frenchmen Drumont and Sorel, and the Germans de Lagarde, Langbehn and Moeller van den Bruck. These members of an emerging proto-fascist intelligentsia in turn drew inspiration from a high caste of philosophers that included Darwin, Wagner, Gobineau, Le Bon, Nietzsche, Dostoyevsky and Bergson [Sternhell in 148: 170]. From these ideological resources fascists constructed an assault on what Sternhell subsumes under the label 'materialism' – the theory of natural rights, of the primacy of the individual, the institutional structure of parliamentary democracy, and the rationalistic foundations of Marxist thought. Crucially, for Sternhell fascism was not directed against Marxism *per se*, but above all against the materialist philosophy that underpinned it. In fact, Sternhell insists that fascism represented an 'antimaterialist and antirationalistic revision of Marxism', and that its first proponents could be found among the revolutionary syndicalists. This leads Sternhell to argue that the fascist ideologies that crystallised in the 1920s represented a synthesis of Left and Right, of 'organic nationalism' with the 'anti-materialist revision of Marxism' [164: p. 8].

By 'tribal nationalism' Sternhell means a nationalism of the *Blut-und-Boden* variety, based on social Darwinism or even notions of biological determinism and racial superiority. This kind of nationalist vision was first advocated by Maurice Barrès, Édouard Drumont, Charles Maurras and Enrico Corradini [164: pp. 10–11]. The first manifestation of this fusion of organic nationalism and revolutionary syndicalism occurred in France, with Maurice Barrès exploiting the violent unrest of the Dreyfus affair to mobilise support for his political campaign in Nancy (Barrès was the first right-wing politician in Europe to use the term 'national socialism'). Yet even before the term was coined, Boulangism had forged the kind of ideological language that Barrès and Sorel would develop into a more elaborate synthesis. This synthesis was possible, Sternhell argues, because both revolutionary syndicalists and radical nationalists were against liberal democracy. Whereas French socialists had defended the bourgeois Republic during the Dreyfus affair, its aftermath saw the emergence of an extreme social-ist Left in both France and Italy that opposed any compromise with liberal-republican regimes. Sternhell points to George Sorel's *Reflections on Violence* (1908), a work that combined nationalism with racist anti-Semitism, as the foremost example of this current of thought [Sternhell in 153: pp. 326–32].

Mussolini, although he was to emerge as the most influential exponent of this ideology, was by no means the only revolutionary syndicalist who converted to radical nationalism. Nor was he the only ex-member of the European Left who after the Great War began to develop a morality and political philosophy that preached violence, condemned liberalism and parliamentary institutions and glorified youth, authority and the strong leader [Sternhell in 153: pp. 334–6]. Mussolini's career as a newspaper editor offers an impressive testimony to his ideological conversion. In 1910, Mussolini the young socialist edited *La Lotta di Classe*. In 1914, by which time he had come to embrace radical nationalism, Mussolini had become the editor of *Il Popolo d'Italia* [Sternhell in 153: p. 336]. Sternhell's argument, that part of the reason for fascism's popular appeal must be sought in this combination of nationalism and socialism, finds confirmation in statements by contemporary observers. As Marcel Déat wrote in September 1940:

> All things considered, I think it comes down to this one observation: the driving force of Revolution has ceased to be class interest, and has become instead the general interest; we have moved on from the notion of class to that of the nation . . . I shall not try to weigh in the scales the parts played in this undertaking by what is national and by what is social, nor to discover whether it was a question of socialising the national or of nationalising socialism. What I do know is that . . . this mixture is, in the best sense of the word, explosive: rich enough to set all the engine-forces of history backfiring. [Sternhell in 153: p. 337]

Political organisation and institutional breakdown

Cultural explanations which trace fascism's roots in the nineteenth century have not remained unchallenged. A particularly concise and profound critique of the culturalist approach can be found in a recent article by Robert O. Paxton. In this essay, Paxton argues that investigations which focus on doctrine, propaganda and symbols tend to be descriptive rather than explanatory because the link between doctrine and action – and particularly between the adoption of a particular ideology and the ability of a movement to gain power – is notoriously ambiguous. Instead, he urges students of fascism to concentrate on 'fascism in action' by examining the process and context in which fascist movements take shape and develop. Instead of focusing on broad ideological currents and continuities, Paxton proposes a developmental typology. Specifically, he distinguishes between five steps:

(a)   the initial creation of fascist movements;
(b)   their rootings as parties in a political system;
(c)   the acquisition of power;
(d)   the exercise of power;
(e)   radicalisation and entropy.

What Paxton considers of particular importance for the success of a fascist movement – i.e., its transformation from movement into regime – are the 'fascists' accomplices and allies'. Whether this transition can occur depends above all on a movement's ability to co-operate, however selectively, with existing political groupings of the conservative right. The nature of their rhetoric is of little importance in this respect. Adopting a comparative perspective, Paxton concludes that fascist movements were most likely to gain power where existing conservative elites were willing 'to work with the fascists', which depended, of course, on the 'reciprocal flexibility on the part of the fascist leaders' towards such elites [160: p. 16]. There are some affinities here with Hans-Ulrich Wehler's explanation of National Socialism, particularly his emphasis on the manipulative role of 'pre-industrial elites' who, in an attempt to prevent further democratic reforms and to keep socialism at bay, entered into ad hoc alliances with groups of the proto-fascist right [100: pp. 985–9, 990–3, 1276–9].

Of course, the fact that Paxton makes no allowance for ideology in general, and for nationalism in particular, creates its own problems. In particular, it makes it difficult to explain why coalitions between conservatives and fascists may occur in the first place, and why certain fascist movements managed to capture the imagination of the wider public rather than remaining confined to the political fringes.

John Breuilly's chapter on fascism in his *Nationalism and the State* offers an answer to these questions. For Breuilly, fascism represents a 'form of radical nationalism'. Unlike most varieties of nationalism in nineteenth-century Europe, which had accommodated liberal and/or conservative ideals, fascism defined itself in opposition to these values. Thus fascism, according to Breuilly, is a 'radical, anti-bourgeois, anti-liberal, anti-marxist movement of national-imperialist integration' [28: p. 290]. Like Paxton, Eley and others, Breuilly is critical of purely ideological explanations of fascism. Nor does he think fascism's success can best be explained by focusing on the aspect of political organisation. For Breuilly, it is the 'breakdown of the regimes which fascists oppose' that is most likely to explain their success. But why does fascism succeed under such conditions? Why did it 'seem to be the only remaining solution'? It is here that Breuilly incorporates ideology and perception into his explanation. Fascist ideology, he contends, was seen as providing a (negative) response to a situation in which neither 'class' nor 'parliamentary and elitist politics' could 'cope with a crisis facing a political system with a new, politically mobilised population' [28: p. 300].

We may sum up the discussion so far by saying that there is no unbridgeable gap separating the accounts of Mosse, Sternhell and Griffin from those of Paxton and Breuilly. For one thing, all the authors discussed insist on the crucial significance of the First World War and its aftermath for the rise of fascism. For another, with the exception of Paxton, who pays virtually no attention to ideology, they all regard nationalist argument as a vital ingredient of fascism. To be sure, the stress on cultural and intellectual factors leads to a rather continuationist account of fascism (Mosse and Sternhell), whereas the focus on political and structural conditions tends to produce a more discontinuous picture (Paxton and Breuilly).

What about the role of nationalism? Here again the difference is one of degree rather than principle. While the exponents of the culturalist approach regard nationalism as an ideology that strengthened fascism's appeal during the inter-war period, a structuralist like Breuilly would argue that it was only when the existing political institutions broke down that radical-imperialist nationalism (his definition of fascism) began to make progress.

Analytical separation

What is striking, however, is how vague the above interpretations remain when it comes to defining the relationship between nationalism and fascism. In part, this is because most tend to view fascism as a special version of nationalism. I would suggest that whereas this perspective may seem plausible on empirical grounds, the quasi-equation of nationalism and fascism hinders rather than helps the explanation of fascism's political success. If, as I have suggested above, we separate the two phenomena analytically, we may then go on to ask which type of nationalism showed a particular affinity to fascism, and under what circumstances. This is the procedure that Anthony D. Smith has proposed [163]. While conceding an often 'close empirical inter-weaving of nationalism and fascism during the interwar period', he rejects what he calls the evolutionary viewpoint in which fascism appears as the logical culmination of nationalism. Neither Herder nor the French revolutionary nationalists, Smith argues against Kedourie and others, can be sensibly linked to the racial ideology of the Nazis [163: p. 43]. Fascism, Smith insists, flourished under the conditions of cultural anomie and widespread status insecurity that characterised the inter-war period. Unlike nationalism, fascism was tied to this particular socio-economic syndrome.

Even on the ideological plane, Smith contends, it is the differences that predominate. While the nationalist core demands are autonomy, unity and identity, fascists emphasise the need for a strong state, glorify the charismatic leader, and subscribe to a cult of violence. Whereas nationalist movements have proved capable of accommodating various other ideologies into the nationalist core, such as liberalism, socialism, populism and imperialism (one might add conservatism), the less flexible and more totalitarian fascists have restricted themselves to imperialism and populism. Differences are also apparent, in Smith's view, with regard to their relation to racism, anti-Semitism, and the role of violence. Although neither nationalism nor fascism is necessarily racist or anti-Semitic, Smith contends that fascism, because of its 'exaltation of power over weakness' and its glorification of mass violence, displays an affinity to racist and anti-Semitic thought that nationalism does not, per se, possess [163: pp. 60, 68].

Homeland nationalism and geopolitical turmoil

In highlighting substantive differences between nationalism and fascism, Smith makes a sensible case for their analytical separation. But if I can see a problem with his highly illuminating chapter on this complex subject, it is that it remains largely confined to the ideal-typical level and does not address the decisive substantive question: which kind of nationalism, and under what conditions, proved histori-cally conducive to fascism's appeal? In what follows I should like to focus on nationalism's role as a potential device for fascist mass mobil-isation. The emphasis will be on the dynamic interaction of ideology (in the sense of well-established nationalist idioms) and geopolitical trans-formations that favour irredentist forms of nationalism. One of the few students of fascism who has insisted on the potentially close causal connection between shifting national boundaries, ethnonationalist struggles in mixed border areas, and the appeal of fascist movements promoting irredentist forms of nationalism is Juan Linz [156: pp. 29–30; Linz in 154: pp. 157–8]. But it is above all the historical sociologist Rogers Brubaker who has pointed to the explosive nationalist dynamics characterising inter-war Europe: 'In interwar Europe, one of the most dangerous fault lines was that along which domestic nationalisms of ethnically heterogeneous nationalizing states collided with the transborder nationalisms of neighbouring "homeland" states, oriented to co-ethnics living as minorities in the nationalizing states' [64: p. 107].

It is those brands of nationalism that display a particular obsession with ethnic unity and racial purity that have historically played a key part in fascist mobilisation. Geopolitical turmoil, manifested in the redrawing of state borders and in the creation of new majority–minority constellations, reinforces this obsession and can turn into the kind of mythical populism and violent aggression that is the hallmark of fascism in action. In the inter-war period, such geopolitical turmoil resulted from the acquisition of substantial minority populations (the Romanian scenario) or from contraction through the loss of both territory and perceived *Volksgenossen* (the Hungarian and German scenarios). Fuelled by these geopolitical explosions, this kind of integral nationalism reached fever pitch in a few societies. It was in this context, that is, once the obsession with the organic nation had become a widespread concern, that fascist ideologues would draw on nationalist arguments to increase the internal coherence and external appeal of their movement. The remainder of this chapter outlines and further discusses this argument, using Germany, Hungary and Romania as the main examples. But before we turn to these cases of fascist mass mobilisation, let us look at two examples of stalled fascist movements: Switzerland and France.

Stalled fascist movements

In Switzerland, the two conditions that proved conducive to fascist mobilisation in Hungary, Romania and Germany – a tradition of strong organic nationalism and geopolitical turmoil after the First World War – were absent. In France, the picture was more ambivalent. Organic nationalism had clearly been present in France from the late nineteenth century, but it had on the whole been kept in check by a strong current of republican, voluntarist nationalism that was firmly institutionalised.

Moreover, France saw its former territory restored after the First World War.

Switzerland

From the late 1920s, developments in Germany and Italy encouraged right-wing mobilisation within Switzerland. In concrete terms, the coincidence of Nazi ascendancy with the economic depression of the early 1930s produced a mushrooming of various political protest groups, most following a radical right-wing agenda [145]. Some of these movements fit the essential criteria of Eley's definition of fascist organisations. They displayed an 'aggressively plebeian style', a 'crude and violent egalitarianism', and the use of 'new propagandist forms and a general invasion of the cultural sphere' to realise their aims [142: p. 270]. This applies in particular to both the Nationale Front and the Neue Front. Founded in 1930, the two movements fused in April 1933 to become the most popular fascist organisation in Switzerland. Possessing strongholds in Zürich, Schaffhausen, Aargau and St Gallen (with branches in Neuchâtel, Geneva and Lausanne), the Nationale Front displayed the classic features of a proto-fascist organisation: it was committed to an anti-liberal, anti-democratic, anti-socialist and anti-Semitic agenda and called for a cultural and spiritual regeneration of the nation through a strong charismatic leader [146: pp. 71, 359]. A number of middle-class protest movements constituted the second current within the right-wing mobilisation of the early 1930s. Groups such as the Neue Schweiz declared their aim to be Switzerland's spiritual and economic renewal. Like other organisations subscribing to a similar ideological programme, its following included self-employed small traders and manufacturers, shopkeepers and craftsmen, as well as lower civil servants [145].

This phalanx of proto-fascist organisations, middle-class protest movements and established conservative parties such as the Catholic Conservatives joined forces from 1934 in an attempt to reorganise society along corporatist lines. The widespread support for a corporatist order resulted in the launching of a plebiscite for the total revision of the Swiss constitution. Its demands included the abolition of proportional representation and the transfer of power from parliament to professional organisations and the federal state's executive. While the initiative's appeal clearly went beyond the fascist right to include the Young Liberals, the Catholic Schweizerische Konservative Volkspartei and the conservative Liberale Partei der Schweiz, 72 per cent of those who voted opposed it at the ballot box on 8 November 1935 [162; 168]. Although some of the radical protest movements survived this political defeat, it nonetheless marked a turning point. By the end of 1935, the right-wing movement for national regeneration had run out of steam, with its most radical exponents finding themselves increasingly isolated and stigmatised. The co-operation of the fascist right with members of the conservative political establishment had broken down.

But the failure of fascism in Switzerland can hardly be attributed solely to the breakdown of the strategic co-operation between conservatives, radical nationalists and proto-fascist organisations after their collective defeat at the ballot box. Nor does the reference to the strength of Switzerland's liberal and democratic traditions and institutions, though it undoubtedly played its part, suffice as an explanation. The limited appeal of National Socialism – and of domestic fascist or proto-fascist organisations – was in important respects a consequence of the widespread rejection of *völkisch* nationalism as preached in Germany. In part, this was because the doctrine of the *Einheit von Volk und Rasse* posed a direct threat to Switzerland's territorial integrity as a polyethnic state. This in turn triggered a Swiss nationalist response that gained momentum from the mid-1930s and undermined the legitimacy of anti-democratic movements of the radical right. This genuinely Swiss brand of cultural nationalism – along with the fact that Switzerland did not experience the collective status deprivation affecting those who had suffered defeat in the First World War and was generally too small to harbour any nationalist-imperialist ambitions anyway – partly explains the limited success of fascist groups at the ballot box. The Swiss *Volksgemeinschaft* was defined in cultural rather than ethnic or racial terms. (In fact, the term *Volksgemeinschaft* acquired considerable prominence among left-of-centre groups in 1930s Switzerland who invoked it to highlight the contrast to the racist *Volksgemeinschaft* of the Nazis [168; 169].)

France

France provides a much more prominent example of stalled fascism. Although fascism eventually failed in France, the country produced many of fascism's leading thinkers and witnessed the formation of several proto-fascist movements before the First World War. By 1924, fascism had developed a considerable potential in France. It was only in the second part of the 1920s that the fascist threat visibly decreased, only to experience a revival of sorts during the German occupation from the

92

summer of 1940. Its extremely anti-Semitic policies notwithstanding, however, Vichy was a regime of right authoritarianism rather than fascism. Genuine French fascists and proto-fascists for the most part remained in the occupied north [161: pp. 398–9].

It is hardly an accident that many of France's most influential fascist writers emerged before the First World War. The Third Republic was born out of the defeat in the war against Prussian-led Germany in 1870. This defeat resulted in the loss of Alsace-Lorraine, which caused a degree of humiliation and status deprivation that was conducive to the emergence of what Stanley Payne has called a 'prefascist situation'. Paul Déroulède's League of Patriots (founded in 1882), the Boulangist movement of 1886–9, and the Action Française (founded in 1899) were all impregnated with a revolutionary nationalism and a rhetoric of national vengeance directed against Germany. Although in the wake of Sedan this revisionist nationalism cut across classes and political affiliations – a nationalism that had its powerful symbol in the 'lost province' of Alsace-Lorraine – its fiercest exponents were on the right. It is therefore hardly an accident that, apart from Paris, right-wing and proto-fascist candidates were particularly successful in the eastern departments of France [see 98: ch. 9].

In the Dreyfus affair (1898–1900) this radical, anti-Semitic and revisionist nationalism clashed head-on with bourgeois-democratic and socialist defenders of the Republic [98: pp. 195–6]. Their defence of the Republic was not based on cosmopolitan rhetoric. Rather, it drew inspiration from a nationalist idiom that had established itself in post-revolutionary France. The French republican counter-nationalism of the late nineteenth century defined national belonging in voluntarist rather than deterministic terms and was uncompromising in its demand for assimilation as a precondition for civil rights. It was centred on values and political institutions rather than on ethnic (or even racial) descent and the soil, the elements that figured so prominently in the rhetoric of right-wing nationalists like Déroulède, Barrès, Drumont, Maurras and Sorel. While the latter subscribed to an organic exclusionary definition of Frenchness in which Jews and others were seen as unassimilable, republican nationalists like Emile Zola adhered to a distinctively assimilationist understanding of French national identity. This understanding, Brubaker tells us, was 'deeply rooted in political and cultural geography and powerfully reinforced in the 1880s by the Republican program of universal primary education and universal military service'. It was also institutionalised through the introduction – by no means an uncontroversial measure at the time – of *jus soli* (acquisition of citizenship by virtue of birth in the territory), first in 1851 and then, in a more extended form, in 1889 [141: pp. 85–6].

But the reference to political and cultural traditions and structures – as embodied by France's democratic institutions along with the salience of an assimilationist and state-centred understanding of national identity – can only be part of an explanation of why right-wing and proto-fascist movements were incapable of crossing the threshold to power in France. Geopolitical factors were equally significant. To begin with, despite her defeat in 1870 and the revanchist nationalism this engendered, France was spectacularly successful as an imperial power, much more so than Germany. This is not to say that by 1900 French imperialists had become saturated and tame in their ambitions. In 1896, Gabriel Honotaux still described world politics as a struggle and a race in which France had to succeed: 'We must create as many Frances as possible both nearby and in distant regions of the world. The issue at stake is to preserve our language, our customs, our ideals, the reputation of France . . . in the midst of a bitter competition with other races which entered upon the same path' [cited in 85: p. 220]. But the Entente Cordiale (1904) put an end to the competition between France and Britain in Africa. More important still, France, albeit at an enormous cost in human life – 1.35 million died and 3.5 million were wounded – was among the victors of the First World War. Most significantly perhaps (besides the fact that the world slump hit France less severely than Germany), France saw her territory restored through the incorporation of Alsace and Lorraine after the war. If we remind ourselves that these two provinces had been a focal point of radical nationalist mobilisation for more than three decades, it seems at least plausible that the outcome of the war played a part in diminishing fascist potential in inter-war France [161: pp. 41–8].

Successful fascist movements

Let us now turn to three cases where fascist movements were successful in mobilising mass support: Germany, Hungary and Romania. It is important to stress that 'success' here is not defined in terms of the ability to establish fascist regimes. Only in Germany (and, of course, Italy) were fascists truly 'successful' in this respect, while in Hungary and Romania their position was more ambivalent and depended considerably on external support, or even active interference by a major

fascist power. However, in both Hungary and Romania fascist movements were successful in mobilising large sections of the public in
national elections.

Romania

When it comes to demonstrating the combined effects of nationalism
and geopolitical turmoil, Romania is a particularly instructive example.
As mentioned in the previous chapter, integral nationalism, underpinned
by a tradition of anti-Semitism, was well established in core Romania
before the First World War. Thus Fischer-Galati sees in the agrarian,
anti-Semitic populism of the nineteenth century the 'forerunners of the
anticapitalist fascists of the interwar era' [144: p. 114]. These ideological currents were further strengthened as a result of Romania's massive
territorial expansion in the aftermath of the war. Although the transition
of the old kingdom into Greater Romania was to the taste of nationalist
imperialists, it also created considerable problems. The acquisition of
substantive minority populations – Hungarians, Germans, Ukrainians,
Russians and Jews – posed a serious threat to the nationalist vision of the
ethnically homogeneous state. At the same time, the Romanian authorities, eager to fight backwardness and catch up with the West, saw their
ambitions threatened by the predominance of the non-ethnic-Romanian
element in important sectors of the economy, education, and cultural life
more generally.

Unlike in late nineteenth-century France, however, where the radical and proto-fascist right was challenged and defeated by a republican
nationalist movement, in Romania official and radical nationalism
reinforced each other. As Livezeanu writes on their relationship:
'Radical nationalist goals, such as the limitation of national minorities
in professional elites and educational institutions, paralleled those of
mainstream nationalists preoccupied with completing Greater
Romania's national consolidation' [Livezeanu in 140: p. 219]. The aim
of the nationalising state was for Romanians to dominate the middle
classes, the key public services and the economy. Given the strength of
the 'foreign' element in Romania's economic and cultural life –
Hungarians, Germans and Jews in particular – this project involved
active discrimination against all these groups. In the nationalist
perspective, these were legitimate measures in a struggle against the
alleged domination of the Romanian people, and the subversion of
their culture and national character, by 'foreigners' [Livezeanu in 140:
pp. 221–2]. Thus while Romania may have benefited from the peace

settlements, the new multi-ethnic reality was widely seen as a threat to the nation's unity, integrity and prosperity.

It is important to avoid an objectivist fallacy here: this sense of crisis and national subversion was not the inevitable product of the redrawing of national boundaries that took place after the war and which led to the creation of Greater Romania – Romania had been an independent state since 1878. It was above all the product of an integral nationalist vision whose champions sought to create a pure and unified Romanian *Volk*. As we saw in the last chapter, however, this ambitious vision was difficult to put into practice. For one thing, Romanian state nationalism triggered what Brubaker has termed 'homeland nationalism', an irredentist counter-nationalism emanating from the revisionist states, particularly Hungary, towards the national minorities that had fallen under Romanian control as a result of the peace treaties [64: p. 110]. The emancipation of the Jews, supported before 1914 by King Carol and other members of the establishment, had no chance of success in Romania's parliament. When Jews were finally granted equal rights in 1919 as a result of external pressure, this was seen as an act of interference in Romania's national affairs and caused considerable resentment [Livezeanu in 140: p. 222; 167: p. 105]. Moreover, in a backward society like Romania where minority populations such as the Hungarians and the Jews played an important role in the urban economy, nationalist ambitions of ethnic Romanian dominance were difficult to satisfy. In this context, the perception of setbacks and failures only served to reinforce nationalist resentment. According to Livezeanu, the charged nationalist climate resulting from these conditions – fuelled by anti-urban sentiments, populism, xenophobia and anti-Semitism – 'favoured the growth of a fascist movement' in Romania [Livezeanu in 140: p. 223]. Fascists like Cuza and Codreanu began to liken Romania to a potentially healthy body that had been infected by foreign mores and customs, selecting the Jews as their prime scapegoats. But the use of biological metaphors in nationalist discourse was not confined to committed fascists. In the 1920s, for example, the Transylvanian poet Octavian Goga described Romania as a 'sick body' beset by 'parasites' and warned of the detrimental effects on national character of a 'wave of foreigners' that was growing ceaselessly, 'like a column of conquerors' [Livezeanu in 140: p. 231].

Once accepted as the new common sense, this nationalism had the effect of lowering the threshold for violent action against the declared 'enemies', if it did not explicitly call for such action. The prevalence of this kind of integral nationalism also helped make violence tolerable. Codreanu was acquitted of murdering the Jassy police prefect in 1924, as were many of those who had organised and taken part in riots against Jews. The trials themselves, as well as the conspicuous lack of intervention by local police, suggests that fascists who committed crimes against Jews enjoyed wide support. These events indicate that, from the mid-1920s, the radical nationalists around the League of National Christian Defence and the later Legion of the Archangel Michael, or Iron Guard, rather than the ruling National Liberals, were calling the shots in the provinces [Livezeanu in 140: pp. 233–6]. The turbulent power struggle between King Carol II and the Iron Guard that took place in the late 1930s testifies to the enormous appeal of fascism in Romania by the outbreak of the Second World War. For although General Antonescu turned decisively against the Iron Guard as that movement threatened to get out of control in the autumn/winter of 1940, the regime he established in January 1941 was still a 'fascist military dictatorship' [144: p. 119].

Hungary

Hungary presents us with the virtual inversion of the Romanian scenario. If the states of Czechoslovakia and Poland were literally created after the First World War, and Romania emerged from it much enlarged, Hungary was the biggest loser in the peace settlement apart from Germany. Whereas the Compromise of 1867 had elevated Hungary to the status of the second power within a large multinational empire, defeat in the war relegated her to a small nation-state. As a result of the Treaty of Trianon (4 June 1920), three-fifths of Hungary's population, including 28 per cent of the Hungarian speakers, were 'lost' to other states. While pre-war Hungary had had a population of close to 21 million, post-Trianon Hungary contained just 7.5 million people. Over 3 million ethnic Hungarians were transferred to neighbouring states, including Romania, Czechoslovakia, and what would later be called Yugoslavia [see Table 8 in the Appendix]. Transylvanian Hungarians in Romania emerged as the largest national minority in Europe [Frank in 166: pp. 227–8]. In economic terms, too, the loss was devastating. Rothschild estimates that Hungary lost 58 per cent of her railroad lines, 60 per cent of her road mileage, 84 per cent of her timber resources, and 83 per cent of her iron ore [129: p. 156].

Hardly surprisingly, the psychological and political effects of the peace settlements on Hungary were profound. As well as symbolising humiliation and national dismemberment, Trianon became a hated symbol of defeat and the focal point of an official revisionist nationalism. Hungarian schoolchildren were brought up reciting the revisionist slogan 'No, no, never' during the entire inter-war period. The rise of Hungarism, a doctrine demanding the creation of a Greater Hungary, was the almost inevitable consequence of this collective experience of humiliation and status deprivation. In 1928, Count Kunó Klebelsberg, Hungary's then Minister for Religion and Education, justified this shift in Hungarian nationalism in an extremely revealing set of essays and lectures. Insisting that Trianon had made the traditional aim of Hungarian nationalism – Magyarisation, i.e. the more or less forced assimilation of non-ethnic Hungarians – obsolete, Klebelsberg called for the creation of a Hungarian 'Neonationalism' as an antidote to the country's deep crisis. While Hungarians had been 'nationalists longer than any other nation living in Europe', he urged them to 'find new aims for old feelings'. Hungarians, Klebelsberg suggested, should strive to become culturally and economically superior to their neighbours. They should endeavour to become 'a racially more important nation' than the 'people living around us' [cited in Frank in 166: pp. 209–10]. Although Klebelsberg did not openly advocate a revisionist agenda of annexation and expansion, the demand for such a policy was implied in his argument. After all, how else was Hungary, reduced as it was in terms of population size and cultural and economic resources, going to achieve regional hegemony?

Yet the watershed of the First World War notwithstanding, it is again important to emphasise the connections between Hungary's revisionist inter-war nationalism and earlier forms of nationalism. In fact, as Frank has emphasised, Hungary went through several phases of nationalist development: from the anti-Habsburg movement aiming at national self-determination, to the anti-minority programme of Magyarisation that lasted from the late nineteenth century to the eve of the First World War, to the aggressive revisionist nationalism of the inter-war period. As we saw in the previous chapter, forced Magyarisation of non-ethnic Hungarians became government policy between 1880 and 1914. Although members of the Hungarian intelligentsia such as Oszkár Jászi criticised this policy, by around 1900 the idea of an 'ethnically pure' Hungarian state had become a widely shared ideal [Frank in 166: p. 223]. The chaotic events of 1918–20 offered a first taste of what was to come after Trianon. The defeat of the central powers (Germany and Austria–Hungary) provoked a Hungarian military offensive against

Romania and Czechoslovakia in the spring and summer of 1919. In the same year, Hungary experienced a communist coup that was quickly put down by a right-wing counter-revolution. These turbulent events were followed by a wave of nationalist and (on a scale unprecedented in the history of Hungary) anti-Semitic outbursts that had the support of the peasant masses and the lower middle classes of the cities who resented the Jews for their prominent role in the professions, in finance and trade, and among the skilled workforce. From 1919 onwards, anti-Semitism became part and parcel of official government policy, and it would soon feature prominently in the propaganda of both the Government Party and, above all, the fascist movement of the Arrow Cross. Intimidation, pogroms and executions were an integral feature of the elections of January 1920, resulting in more than 5000 victims, many of them Jewish [129: pp. 171, 177–8; Ránki in 154: p. 408].

Right-wing nationalists and fascists of the inter-war period could build on the central premise of the policy of Magyarisation: that the Hungarian state was the property of the ethnic Hungarians and that Hungary was a one and indivisible nation. Given the new situation of post-Trianon Hungary, this ethnic nationalism was transformed in two directions. First, and reflecting the fact that post-Trianon Hungary had become much more homogeneous in ethnic terms, the Jews became the preferred domestic target of Hungarian nationalism. Second, given the fact that millions of ethnic Hungarians had come under 'foreign rule' – above all in Greater Romania and in the newly created Czechoslovakia – organic Hungarian nationalism became expansionist and aggressive. This new nationalism was conducive to the rise of Hungarian fascism, which had its most powerful champion in the Arrow Cross [129: pp. 171–7].

Based on an agenda of anti-capitalism, anti-socialism, anti-Semitism and racism, the Arrow Cross recruited its leadership above all from army officers and civil servants [Lacko in 154: p. 395]. By the end of 1938 the movement, no doubt benefiting from German financial assistance and encouraged by the success of Nazi foreign policy (the *Anschluss* of Austria was followed by the occupation of Czechoslovakia), had become a real political force with a membership of approximately 300,000. It derived its main support from students, unskilled workers and sections of the industrial proletariat, the lower middle classes of the towns and villages, and from agricultural labourers. The Arrow Cross proved capable of mobilising these groups, including significant sections of workers in Budapest who lacked political organisation due to the weakness of the Socialist Party and the banning of the Communist Party. In the 1939 parliamentary elections, the movement received a quarter of the votes polled nationally, which was double the socialist vote and relatively close to the vote of the Government Party. Its unprecedented success also helped push the ruling Government Party further to the right [129: pp. 180–2; Lacko in 154: pp. 395–7; Ránki in 154].

To be sure, Hungarian fascism's success at regime level was ambiguous and short-lived. The Government Party remained in office to 1944; by then the Arrow Cross was in serious decline and divided. It was only German interference that allowed it a brief tenure of power in 1944 because Hitler felt Horthy had betrayed him and installed the Arrow Cross in office. Even so, the electoral appeal of fascism in Hungary was considerable during the 1930s, and it was closely linked to a revisionist nationalism that enjoyed wide currency during the inter-war period. Revisionism was the central determining factor in Hungary's foreign policy. Hungarian nationalists felt an elective affinity with the revisionist powers of Italy and Germany that went beyond strategic considerations. Hungary's leadership concluded treaties with Mussolini's fascist Italy in 1927, followed by an agreement with Nazi Germany in the summer of 1933 [Frank in 166: p. 229]. In 1935, moreover, the Hungarian prime minister Gömbös signed a secret agreement with Goering in which he promised to establish in Hungary a political system modelled on the Third Reich. After the *Anschluss* in 1938 Hungary introduced anti-Semitic laws along Nazi lines, although the Government Party was extremely reluctant to implement them in spite of considerable German pressure. It was only in March 1944, when the Nazis established a puppet government of the extreme right in Hungary, that the concentration of Jews in ghettos and camps occurred that prepared the ground for their systematic deportation to Nazi extermination camps [see Tilkovszky in 165].

The return of southern Slovakia and Ruthenia in 1938 (then part of Czechoslovakia) and part of Transylvania in 1940 (then part of Romania) to Hungary was the reward for Hungary's alliance with the Axis powers [Frank in 166: p. 230; 129: pp. 179, 183–4]. But these gains would be eradicated when the German offensive in the East came to a halt and the offensive of the Red Army began in 1943.

Germany

In inter-war Germany, the success of National Socialism in the election of 1933 dealt the final blow to the besieged Weimar Republic. But even in this most prominent of fascist takeovers there was continuity amidst the discontinuity. Even if we accept that the outcome of the First World War was decisive for the radicalisation of nationalism that provided a basis for fascist mobilisation – and there can be no doubt that it was – these continuities need not be overlooked. The outcome of the war and the consequences of defeat had the effect of radicalising existing nationalist dispositions and narratives – they did not in themselves invent them [see Eley in 140: p. 57].

The debate and practice surrounding national citizenship is particularly significant in this respect. Comparatively restrictive definitions of national membership along ethnic lines had already evolved in the late nineteenth century, reaching their institutional solidification immediately before the First World War. To be sure, all late nineteenth-century states, including France and Britain, granted citizenship on the basis of ethnic descent (or *jus sanguinis*, to employ the legal term). Descendants of French or British nationals acquired the national citizenship of their parents, even if they were born outside French or British territory. The more significant question concerns the degree of allowance made for *jus soli* – the acquisition of national membership through birth in the territory. As recent research by Gosewinkel and Fahrmeir has shown, in this respect Germany only began to differ from the French and British models in the two decades preceding the First World War. Before that, restrictive definitions of membership were determined by municipalities and individual states rather than by the imperial government. Many of them displayed an eagerness to restrict immigration not just with respect to non-German nationals, but also with respect to immigrants from other German states, an inclination that was above all related to issues of poor relief and regulating the relations between various German states [for a critique of Brubaker's influential account, see 112 and 143].

Yet a conspicuous shift occurred after 1871, a shift that affected both the public debate and institutional practice on national citizenship. From the late nineteenth century naturalisation was increasingly denied on ethnic grounds. In the 1880s, this tendency became manifest in the 1885 law initiated by the Prussian Minister of the Interior, Puttkammer. As we saw in the last chapter, this law, along with other pieces of legislation concerning the minorities in eastern Prussia, was clearly directed against Poles and Polish Jews. Applications for citizenship, especially by Jews from eastern Europe, had virtually no chance of success. Prussia led the way in this respect, but from the 1890s the Prussian practice became prevalent throughout the German *Reich* [124: p. 133].

The introduction of *jus sanguinis* at national level in the *Reichs- und Staatsangehörigkeitsgesetz* of 1913 was supported by all major political parties except the Social Democrats and the Fortschrittliche Volkspartei who supported a qualified version of *jus soli* along French lines. Shortly before the final vote, the conservative delegate Ernst Giese expressed his satisfaction about the legislation: 'We welcome the fact that . . . ethnic descent and affiliation of blood form the guiding principles when it comes to granting citizenship rights. This principle is best suited to maintaining and conserving the German *völkisch* character' [cited in 124: p. 134].

Moreover, recent research on nationalism within popular associations before the First World War suggests that this organic and essentialist understanding of the nation in terms of a *Volk* was not confined to the political class. The German choir societies, for example, explicitly emphasised that the German *Volk* could not be confined to the borders of the *Reich*. Quite the contrary, they made it their task 'to further the unity of all Germans in conformity with their old traditions'. The choir societies – not just the radical nationalists – were very much concerned with the question of Germans living abroad. The Austrian, the Sudeten German, even the Swiss choir societies, all received invitations to take part in the annual main events because they were seen as part of one German *Volk*, and of one German nation. Whether implicitly or explicitly, irredentism became part and parcel of the German folk song movement well before the outbreak of the First World War [87: p. 143]. Svenja Goltermann, in her recent account of the German gymnast societies, observes a shift towards an ethnic conception of German nationhood in the *Turner* movement after 1871, which manifested itself in a strong preoccupation with Austria. While the German 'nation' tended to be associated with the newly created state, the German *Volk* was seen in ethnic and thus trans-state terms [75: pp. 222–4].

These understandings of nationhood were politicised and radicalised at the beginning of the twentieth century. According to Eley, we can distinguish two phases in the formation of a radical nationalism before the First World War. In a first phase, we witness the genesis of a 'dissident and largely anti-parliamentary radical nationalist public' (1890–1908). The nationalism underpinning this movement showed a strong concern with the fate of ethnic Germans abroad – with the German national minorities in Austria, in Bohemia, in the Baltic, and in Hungary – who were portrayed as under threat. This was linked to calls for national consolidation of the entire German *Volkstum* in a Greater

Germany. Among the nationalist pressure groups promoting this agenda were the Pan-German League (1891), the Society for the Eastern Marches (1894), the Navy League (1898), the Imperial League against Social Democracy (1904), and the Army League (1912). Although most of these movements remained relatively small in terms of their membership, some managed to attract a considerable following. The Navy League, for example, had a total membership of 331,000 on the eve of the First World War, and its links with government secured it a degree of influence that was not reflected in its size [Eley in 140].

In the years immediately preceding the outbreak of the war, this radical right was reintegrated into the 'right-wing mainstream', which after the Second Moroccan Crisis (1911) adopted an increasingly expansionist and imperialist line. As Eley comments on this transformation of the political landscape: 'During the radicalisation of 1912–1920 the Pan-German panacea – the idea of a unified race-people mobilized for battle with internal and external foes, obliterating the divisiveness of class-sectional, particularist and confessional loyalties via the fanatical pursuit of German aggrandizement – entered the discourse of the right as a whole' [Eley in 140: p. 64]. The outbreak of the First World War offered an opportunity to put this programme into practice, particularly after the victories in the East, only to be frustrated by the final defeat in 1918. The profound socio-political turmoil that followed – embodied in the Kaiser's abdication, the revolutionary threat, the gains of the Left in national elections, and the massive territorial losses – meant that the Pan-German and radical nationalists had now fully marginalised the traditional Conservatives [Eley in 140: pp. 61, 64–5].

While during the German Empire (1871–1918) the authorities had managed to contain 'homeland nationalism', after the war, as millions of Germans became members of national minorities and found themselves exposed to the nationalising pressures of the successor states – the Baltic German Ewald Ammende, a leading proponent of the concept of cultural autonomy, 'believed that 8,996,000 out of 80 million Germans lived as minorities around the continent' [151: p. 448] – this proved increasingly difficult, if not impossible. Thus one of the reasons why the Weimar Republic lacked legitimacy in the eyes of many Germans was its association with a weakened German nation-state allegedly incapable of protecting its ethnic population. Both Austrians and the majority of Germans wished the *Anschluss* of Austria to Germany after the war [116: pp. 61–2]. The Weimar National Assembly voted unanimously in favour of incorporating the Austrians into the German *Reich*. The French government, fearful of an enlarged and invigorated Germany, intervened to prevent this from happening. The German government had no alternative but to comply, adding yet more fuel to German nationalist resentment. It also favoured the proliferation of new pressure groups devoted to an expansionist nationalist agenda during the Weimar period. These included the Association of Germandom Abroad (2 million members), the German Protective League for Border and Foreign Germandom, the Organisation of German Ethnonational Groups in Europe, as well as various youth and church associations advocating the same cause. As Brubaker describes the nationalist dynamic of the Weimar period: 'These "heroic" struggles in the ethnic borderlands helped divert nationalists' attention from the "impotent" state to the vigorous, autonomous *Volk*' [64: p. 119; on the non-irredentist minority organisation initiated by Ewald Ammende in the 1920s, see 151].

A flood of literature on the subject of *Ostforschung* was published at academic and pseudo-academic levels. All these groups and individuals regarded the German national minorities abroad as ethnic frontier groups whose resettlement was to be opposed and prevented at all cost. But even where this failed it was not necessarily detrimental to the revisionist cause. Resettlers from Poland – around 65 per cent of the ethnic German population had left Poland for Germany by the mid-1920s – played a key role in the *Deutschtumspolitik* of the Weimar era and supplied an important contingent of Nazi supporters. To some extent, this also applies to resettlers from the Baltic states, the Sudetenland, and the formerly Russian and Austro-Hungarian territories [64: pp. 117–36]. Following the *Anschluss* of Austria in 1938, most Habsburg officers served Nazi Germany, and 'more than 300 former Habsburg career officers reached the rank of general in the Wehrmacht or the Waffen SS' [107: p. 134].

In an important sense, then, the National Socialists were the true beneficiaries of Weimar homeland nationalism, a nationalism they had actively promoted ever since their organisation had been founded. As Brubaker has argued, they appropriated its *völkisch* idioms and its notion of *Lebensraum*, its network of official and semi-official agencies and organisations. Hitler expressed thus this obsession with the supposedly unchanging quality of the *Volk*: 'Estates vanish, classes change, human fate evolves, something remains throughout and must remain: The Volk as a substance of flesh and blood' [cited in 87: p. 102]. The Nazis also used the staunchest advocates of such nationalist convictions among the German frontier groups – the national minorities in Poland and the self-declared champions of

Germandom in the Sudetenland – to destroy the Polish and Czechoslovak states. The German ambassador in Czechoslovakia estimated that by the end of 1933 about 2 million of the 3 million Sudeten Germans were Nazi sympathisers [152: pp. 128–9].

Domestically, too, there is reason to assume that the Nazis' expansive nationalist rhetoric paid political dividends, particularly in borderland areas. Thus a glance at the ten districts most supportive of the National Socialists in the Reichstag elections between 1930 and 1933 reveals that more than half represented such geographic areas. Districts like East Prussia, Pomerania, Schleswig-Holstein, Chemnitz Zwickau and Frankfurt Oder were consistently amongst the National Socialists' strongest supporters. Even among predominantly Catholic regions, which on the whole were considerably less supportive of the Nazi Party, the border districts reveal a certain deviation from this pattern. The two districts of Breslau and Liegnitz, for example, located in the predominantly Catholic yet industrialised region of Silesia with its legacy of anti-Polish agitation, displayed much stronger support for the Nazis than other Catholic regions. The same applies to the predominantly rural and Catholic Palatinate, which experienced a wave of nationalist revival in the 1920s in the wake of French intervention [for detailed statistics and comments on these elections, see 159: pp. 81–3].

To sum up the argument presented in this chapter: nationalism provided but one of several factors which contributed to the rise of fascist movements, but one that has rarely been explored systematically by students of fascism. The emphasis throughout has been on how fascist movements used specific nationalist arguments to gain mass political support even in those countries where they did not succeeed in capturing the state and creating their own regime. Fascist movements, where they proved a significant force in national elections – as they did in Germany, Hungary and Romania from the 1930s (and a decade earlier in Italy) – benefited from the social, economic and political crisis of inter-war Europe. Specifically, it was the combination of nationalism and geo-political turmoil characterising east central Europe during this period that provided a seedbed for fascist mobilisation. This region witnessed a clash between the nationalising nationalisms of states like Poland, Romania and Czechoslovakia and the homeland nationalisms of defeated states like Hungary and Germany. While this fateful dynamic could build on pre-war (institutionalised) traditions of organic and integral nationalism, it was their radicalisation after 1918 that turned them into a mobilising resource for fascist movements. For the leaders and supporters of a powerful fascist state like Germany, open threats and expansionist warfare were equally legitimate means to realise revisionist and expansionist aims. One ought to recall that the first states that were annexed through such means by Nazi Germany – Czechoslovakia, Austria, Poland and France – had been explicit targets of German homeland nationalism ever since the peace treaties had been signed.

5 Universalism Reconsidered: Nationalism and its Critics

The explorations so far may have created the impression that nationalism was more or less irresistible. This impression is only partly accurate, particularly if we extend our chronological and geographical focus. This final chapter examines how conservative, liberal and socialist thinkers and movements perceived nationalism. This will reveal that the only political camp that opposed nationalism unreservedly was political conservatism. Liberals and socialists did not on the whole reject nationalist doctrines but sought to integrate them into their own thought world. In practice, they attempted to accommodate nationalist arguments and use them to buttress their own political goals.

Classic conservative critiques of nationalism

Apart from the not very numerous cosmopolitans and anarchists of various forms, perhaps the most consistent critics of nationalism have been classic conservatives. One of the first and most powerful critics of nationalism was the great conservative thinker Edmund Burke. In his *Reflections on the Revolution in France* (1790), Burke defended the English system against what he perceived as the dangerous new creed invented in revolutionary France. Against the positive emphasis on novelty and creation, Burke held the principles of inheritance and organic communal growth. According to Burke, states and the moral values and laws that sustained them, having evolved over centuries in accordance with the law of nature, ought not to be changed at will. These values and traditions defined 'a partnership not only between those who are living, but between those who are living, those who are dead, and those who are to be born' [Burke in 1: pp. 134–42]. Writing more than half a century after Burke's reflections, Lord Acton formulated a similar critique of modern nationalism. Turning his attention to the Habsburg Empire, Acton saw nationalism as a threat to the traditional legitimacy of the state. But Acton directed his critique not only at nationalism but also at the rulers of traditional dynastic states. Nationalism was most likely to emerge as a destructive political force where the traditional rulers had failed or committed gross injustices against their subject populations. Thus in Acton's view, the Pandora's box of nationalism had been opened by an act of despotism. It was the unlawful partition of Poland, he insisted in his essay on 'Nationality', that had dealt the death blow to the 'ancient European system' and thus enabled the rise of a 'new world' in which the 'principle of nationality would hold sway' [Acton in 10: p. 21].

As an admittedly broad generalisation, we can thus conclude that conservative thinkers and politicians have on the whole been opposed to nationalism because it posed a threat to the traditional order – an order based on ascribed (rather than achieved) status and patriarchal rule, and one which some conservatives (Acton, but not Burke) saw as God-given. Another reason why many conservatives were wary of nationalism lies in its strong affinity with populism and extensive forms of democracy based on popular sovereignty. Some, particularly religious conservatives, also resented the secularising thrust that is inherent in most nationalist movements. All these elements threatened to undermine the authority of the kind of order with which conservatives identified and in whose preservation they had a vested interest. The protracted conflict between conservatives and those who embraced the revolutionary legacy in France – a conflict that has continued to the present day – has centred on questions concerning the sources of authority and legitimate rule. The same schism can be observed in post-unification Germany and other countries in central and eastern Europe, where conservative elites (rather than liberals who by the late nineteenth century had shifted to the right of the political spectrum) tried to defend their status by opposing nationalism. This is not to say that conservatives did not embrace 'the nation' as a focus of loyalty and allegiance. But they clearly distinguished between the nation conceived as a cultural or status community and the political nation as defined by modern nationalists. [The relationship between conservative thought and politics and nationalism has found little systematic attention. Some useful insights can be gained from the following works: 181: pp. 71–7; 53; 98: chs. 9 and 11.]

Liberals and nationalism in practice

Mainstream liberals expressed far fewer reservations about nationalism than classic conservatives. In fact, liberals were the earliest and strongest supporters of nationalist arguments. It was particularly between 1830 and 1848, Stuart Woolf has asserted, that 'political nationalism (as distinct from cultural expressions of national consciousness, without a political programme) [became] intimately associated with liberalism'. In part, this strong association of liberalism and nationalism finds its explanation in the fact that 'the anti-liberal states – Prussia, Austria, and Russia – were also anti-national' [19: p. 12; the close links between nationalism and liberalism are emphasised in most general accounts of the subject: 39: ch. 4; 9: ch. 3; a particularly useful survey can be found in 181: pp. 86–101].

Yet depending on where they positioned themselves politically, liberals subscribed to different nationalist arguments. Until the mid-nineteenth century and beyond, moderate liberals in Germany, Switzerland and Italy used the language of unification nationalism to legitimate their calls for constitutional progress and tighter institutional (political and economic) integration at the federal level. This project, they argued, was an embodiment of the progressive spirit that the modern age demanded; better still, it was also in the interest of 'the fatherland' and 'the nation' because it enhanced its international status and prestige. Moderate liberals, who on the whole were not in favour of extending the franchise, did not embrace the concept of popular sovereignty, a concept that had been at the heart of the nationalism of the French Revolution. [Where universal manhood suffrage was introduced early, as in France in 1848, moderate liberals accepted the republican doctrine of popular sovereignty out of pragmatism rather than conviction. See 170.]

Republican radicals, on the other hand, while sharing some of these arguments and ideological strategies, embraced a somewhat different brand of nationalism. These groupings placed the stress on popular sovereignty and national self-determination, reflecting their task of mobilising those sections of the public that had social grievances and demanded an extension of participation rights. Rejecting the liberal viewpoint that the 1815 settlement, in which Switzerland was defined as a loose confederation of cantons, could only be changed through legal means, radicals mobilised the public in the name of national unity. The 'sovereign people', they repeatedly declared, would find their appropriate voice in the 'sovereign nation' [see 170; 180: chs. 8 and 9].

A pressing and crucial problem facing liberals, particularly once the key objective of independent nation-statehood had been achieved, was that the boundaries of nation and state did rarely coincide. Who would determine the political agenda where various ethnic or national groups lived within the same territory? This is the question John Stuart Mill addressed in his essay on 'Nationality' (1861). Mill noted that, quite frequently, 'different nationalities are so locally intermingled that it is not practicable for them to be under separate governments'. It was under such conditions that the normally fruitful alliance of liberalism and nationality threatened to break down, destroying free government in its train. Mill's proposed solution was assimilation to the culture of the more 'civilised and cultivated people'. Thus there was no doubt, in Mill's view, that the Bretons or Basques of French Navarre would greatly benefit from becoming full and equal members of 'the French nationality'. The same applied, he continued, to the 'Welshman or the Scottish Highlanders', who would gain from becoming 'members of the British nation' [Mill in 19: p. 44]. The true problem would arise only where the 'more civilised nationality' was in a minority or where 'the nationalities which have been bound together are nearly equal in numbers' [Mill in 19: p. 46]. In the former case, i.e. where the smaller but more civilised nationality prevailed, there was a danger of despotism, while its absorption 'in the less advanced people' would be a loss to civilisation. In the latter case, i.e. where the nationalities were roughly equal in numbers, Mill envisaged a scenario of nationalist strife and calls for separatism [Mill in 19: pp. 46–7].

As Mark Mazower has rightly argued in his account of Europe's twentieth century, Mill's liberal viewpoint stands for the 'Anglo-French belief in assimilationism' – a belief, he noted, that 'only made sense viewed within their national borders' [121: p. 57]. Liberals of Mill's conviction were against the mixing of different nationalities within the same polity because they believed that this would (almost inevitably) undermine the liberal state [for a similar viewpoint, see 179]. Let us accept, for the sake of argument, that the concept of the nationalising state 'made sense' in France and Britain. (Many members of the groups Mill placed at the receiving end of the 'civilising mission' of the majority groups in charge of the state would, quite understandably, disagree.) What is clear is that assimilationist majority nationalism becomes largely unfeasible if transposed to the different conditions of central and eastern Europe, where ethnolinguistic differences and the complicated territorial intermingling of majority and minority groups were the rule rather than the exception. As we have seen, Hungarian nationalism after the Compromise of 1867

110

was clearly inspired by the kind of view Mill had expressed. The Magyars had held a dominant position within the Habsburg Empire, and they were the majority group within the newly created Hungarian state. Magyarisation – the forced assimilation of Germans, Jews, Slovaks, Romanians and other minority groups – was thus in principle consistent with the liberal assimilationist nationalism that Mill condoned.

The German national movement of the second half of the nineteenth century, in which liberal Protestants formed the overwhelming majority, offers another instructive example. Although Bismarckian power politics and a succession of wars played a decisive part in the unification of the German states, there can be little doubt that the liberal movement was the driving ideological force behind the small-German solution that was realised in 1871 [171; 178: pp. 254–5; 100; 173: pp. 16–17, 51–2]. Once unification had been achieved, right-wing liberals, in tandem with a conservative Prussian elite, proved highly susceptible to integral forms of nationalism. They began to develop a preoccupation with Germany's cultural and ethnic homogeneity within the state's territory. In the liberal (and Protestant) nationalist vision, cultural and institutional homogeneity stood for progress, while pluralism represented backwardness. Nipperdey has noted the 'anti-pluralist turn' among German liberals at the end of the 1870s and their craving for 'consensus and homogeneity' [88, vol. 2: p. 265]. Those who did not share their assimilationist vision – such as the majority of Catholics, Poles and socialists – and those who were perceived as resisting it – such as the Jews – were declared enemies of the nation. Now in charge of the state and its institutional apparatus, liberals (with the help of Protestant conservatives like Bismarck) sought to 'create a homogenous culture across lines of confession' [53: p. 8]. The *Kulturkampf* of the 1870s against Catholic culture and institutions, although initiated by Bismarck, had its most fervent supporters in the National Liberals who resented Catholics' opposition to the state's secularising crusade [88, vol. 2: pp. 364–81].

Right-wing liberals also played a conspicuous role in the anti-Semitic agitation of the late 1870s and 1880s. The prominent historian Heinrich von Treitschke, in a pamphlet that appeared in the *Preussische Jahrbücher*, argued that the Jews dominated the German public and warned of the threat of Jewish immigration from eastern Europe. Treitschke criticised the alleged unwillingness of Jews to assimilate to German culture, an accusation he tried to substantiate by pointing to the relatively low numbers of conversions to Christianity. There was 'no room on German soil', Treitschke exclaimed, 'for double-nationality'.

For Treitschke, the German nation was not only in crisis, it was also under threat, involved in a struggle against internal enemies. Several of Treitschke's professorial colleagues at the University of Berlin signed a protesting note condemning his views. What is interesting, however, is that even those who opposed Treitschke's anti-Semitism – including Theodor Mommsen, who emerged as Treitschke's leading opponent in the so-called *Antisemitismusstreit* – tended to insist that Jewish assimilation into the culture of the national majority had to make further progress. The liberal nationalist vision of the homogenous nation supplied the ideological platform for both anti-Semites and their opponents. While the former used it to dress their hostility towards Jews in the garb of civilised rationality and evolutionary progress, the latter did so because they regarded it as the pillar of the future nation-state. To cite Nipperdey's argument about the intricate and fateful link between nationalism and German right-wing liberalism: 'In a sense, this liberal-national, secular-Protestant idea did not leave room for a plurality of identities, for the continuation of Jewish particularity' [88, vol. 2: p. 294].

Socialism and nationalism

Contrary to common wisdom, there were few socialist thinkers who unanimously rejected nationalism, even though most regarded it as a transitory phenomenon. In fact, socialist and Marxist thinkers produced by far the most sophisticated analyses of nationalism and the nationality question. While liberals and conservatives frequently resorted to highly normative arguments to justify their condemnation or endorsement of nationalism, some leading exponents of the socialist movement developed demanding explanations of a phenomenon that posed a challenge to Marxist class reductionism and economic determinism. It is hardly an accident that most of them – Karl Kautsky, Karl Renner, Otto Bauer, Victor Adler, or Lenin – came from central or eastern Europe, where the explosive force of nationalism had revealed itself decades before the First World War [176; 177; see also 174]. It is therefore justified in my view to deal with the relationship between socialism and nationalism at somewhat greater length.

Marxists and the nation: between rejection and strategic endorsement

Marx and Engels tended to regard the discourse of nationality as an ideology that reflected the interests of the dominant class and thus served as a justification for capitalism. Yet Engels in particular believed that, in certain cases, nationalism could be used to the advantage of the working classes and accelerate their liberation from capitalist domination. While in the large and economically and culturally advanced nation-states such as France and Germany Engels saw nationalism as the ideology of the dominant class, he regarded it as a legitimate and effective weapon if used against imperial domination. As he wrote in 1875: 'I shall always regard the liberation of Poland as being one of the foundation stones of the ultimate liberation of the European proletariat and, in particular, of the liberation of the other Slav nationalities' [cited in 177: p. 48].

Perhaps the fiercest opponent of nationalism among Marxist thinkers was Rosa Luxemburg (1871–1919). Of Jewish–Polish descent, Luxemburg clearly recognised the political significance of the nationality question. Even in Russia, she noted, nationalism had become a firm ingredient of political struggle after the 1905 revolution: 'All the newly formed or forming parties in Russia, be they radical, liberal, or reactionary, have been forced to include in their programs some sort of a position on the nationality question' [Luxemburg in 1: p. 198]. But Luxemburg was fiercely opposed to granting the nationalities within Russia the right to political self-determination, a right that the Social Democratic Labor Party (RSDLP) of Russia endorsed in its party programme and which she perceived as an expression of utopia and anarchism. For Luxemburg, small states based on nationalist principles would inevitably inhibit the transformation to socialism. Nations, in her view, had no real existence outside the bourgeois imagination. As she put it bluntly: 'In a class society, "the nation" as a homogeneous sociopolitical entity does not exist' [Luxemburg in 1: p. 203]. Unlike other Marxist thinkers, Luxemburg was therefore against the creation of a Polish state [Luxemburg in 1: p.199]. Specifically, she argued that an independent Polish state would result in the erection of a tariff barrier between Poland and Russia, which would return Poland to a previous state of development. Poland, she insisted, had hitherto benefited from its close connection to the Russian market. National independence, in contrast, would benefit the reactionary forces while playing against the interest of the socialist working class [111: p. 89].

Hardly surprisingly, Luxemburg's analysis of the Polish question – not least because it was in open contradiction to the position endorsed by the Second International at its 1896 London Congress, that all nations had a right to self-determination – aroused bitter controversies not only among Polish socialists, but also among the various socialist movements in Austria–Hungary. Karl Kautsky, for example, replied that it was unrealistic to downplay the emotional pull of linguistic nationalism. Victor Adler and Leonhard Bernstein were also among the critics of Luxemburg's position on Poland [111: pp. 83–94; 177: pp. 69–70; 138: pp. 138–9].

Lenin's perspective on the nationality question – expressed most cogently in his essay *The Right of Nations to Self-Determination* (first published in 1914) – was closer to Engels's and diverged in important respects from Luxemburg's position. Moving away from materialist determinism and stressing the importance of political action, Lenin saw the principle of national self-determination as legitimate in certain cases. Under conditions of relative economic backwardness, nationalism, so Lenin believed, could serve as a catalyst for a revolutionary transformation [177: p. 87; 111: p. 75]. Implicitly turning against Luxemburg's economic determinism, he wrote: 'To accuse the supporters of freedom of self-determination, i.e., freedom to secede, of encouraging separatism, is as foolish and as hypocritical as accusing the advocates of freedom of divorce of wishing to destroy family ties' [Lenin in 1: p. 212]. But the fact that Lenin thought national movements to be a legitimate and even productive force in certain conditions does not mean that he condoned nationalism, let alone that he saw it as the wave of the future. Once the universalist Marxist vision of the classless society had been achieved, nationalism would lose both its function and its legitimacy. As Forman put it: 'In effect, Lenin simultaneously closed and opened the door for nationalism' [111: p. 82].

Austrian socialism and the nationality question

But it was the Austrian socialists who developed the most sophisticated and complex reflections on nationalism and the nationality question. It was in Cisleithania that these issues had come to dominate politics after the *Ausgleich* of 1867 between Austria and Hungary, acquiring a new intensity with the 1897 conflict over language rights. At its 1899 congress in Brno, the Austrian Socialist Party (Gesamtpartei) responded to this situation by accepting a resolution demanding that Austria be transformed into an autonomous and multinational federal state ('demokratischer Nationalitäten-Bundesstaat'). The resolution envisaged that the historic Crownlands be replaced by self-governing nationalities and insisted that the right of minorities should be protected. The demand for a single official language was rejected [for details of the resolution, see 3: pp. 73–5].

These conflicts provided the inspiration for an intense intellectual engagement with the nationality question by the two leading Austrian socialist thinkers of their time, Karl Renner and Otto Bauer. Both were members of the Austrian Social Democratic Party, and both turned against doctrinal Marxism. It was, as Hans Mommsen has aptly noted, the existential threat that nationalism posed to the Austrian Social Democrat Party that largely explains why it was this organisation that produced its leading theorists [176: p. 201]. Karl Renner's book *Der Kampf der Österreichischen Nationen um den Staat* (published in 1902 under a pseudonym) argued that nationalities were constitutive for the formation of states. Nationalities, according to Renner, were more than the aggregates of individuals. He saw them as cultural communities based on shared sentiment and common patterns of thought. It was only by giving them institutional recognition, he believed, that national tension and conflict could be prevented. Renner was keen to separate 'nation' from 'state', culture from territory, an idea that found expression in the concept of the 'personality principle'.

Within a federalist framework, corporations defined in terms of nationality rather than territory would become the most important administrative units in an attempt to separate mixed populations for the practice of government. The idea was that, within a future Austro-Habsburg federation, people would be entitled to choose which national community to opt into irrespective of where they resided within its territory. As Renner put it in 1902: 'We must separate national and political affairs. . . . We must organise the population twice; once along the lines of nationality, the second time in relation to the state' [cited from Stargardt in 14: p. 91; on the personality principle, see also 111: p. 107; 176: p. 198].

Building on Renner's thoughts, Otto Bauer developed a much more systematic account of nationality in his *Die Sozialdemokratie und die Nationalitätenfrage* (first published in 1907). Like Renner, Bauer regarded nationality as a historical rather than a primordial category. Nations, for Bauer, were not rooted in nature or ethnic descent, let alone biology. Following an analytic logic that closely resembles the later theories of Karl W. Deutsch and Ernest Gellner, Bauer regarded nationalities as the product of far-reaching sociological transformations. More specifically, he argued that it was the close interaction which capitalism engendered – interaction through the medium of a common language –

that had gradually given rise to a 'national character'. Language, according to Bauer, was the 'great medium of interaction'. It was the need for such interaction that generated a common language. If there had been stronger links of interaction between English and German workers, they would have evolved a single language; but as things stood, he contended, there was more intensive interaction between the English bourgeoisie and the English working class, and between the German bourgeoisie and the German working class, than between the similar social classes of the two countries [Bauer in 10: pp. 43–8]. This interaction had produced nations, which Bauer defined as *Schicksalsgemeinschaften* – 'communities of fate' [Bauer in 10: p. 52]. While nations and their characters were open to change, they were nevertheless forming real cultural communities with political ambitions. Nationality, in Bauer's view, was not just a matter of choice but in part determined people's actions. As he noted: 'The nation as a community of character governs the action of its individual members even if they are not aware of their nationality' [Bauer in 10: p. 61].

Bauer recognised more openly than many others that the cultural and institutional hegemony of one dominant group over substantial minority groups was the pattern that caused so much national strife in large states like Austria–Hungary, Russia or Prussia. Ignoring the legitimate quest for recognition and cultural autonomy of the smaller nationalities in the name of internationalism, Bauer was convinced, would only serve to strengthen political nationalism among these groups [111: p. 106]. He hoped that socialism would gradually evolve as a federation of nation-states in which no nationality would dominate the overall institutional framework [176: p. 202]. Even so, neither Bauer nor Renner, whatever their proclamations in favour of national autonomy, were free of the belief in the superiority of the Germans and the desirability of assimilating the smaller nationalities. Both men, moreover, like the majority of the Austrian Social Democrats (and indeed like other leading socialist thinkers such as Victor Adler and Friedrich Engels), advocated Austria's absorption into a greater Germany [176: pp. 212, 216].

As we now know, Renner's and Bauer's theoretical reflections on nationality grew out of the serious concern that the application of classical nationalist argument would spell disaster within the Austrian multinational state. How effective were their ideas in shaping socialist political reality? The answer to this question is rather depressing. Bauer's and Renner's personality principle was never implemented. Co-operation between different nationalities failed even at the level of socialist party organisation within the empire. From 1900 onwards, German and Czech socialists began to fall out over a whole range of issues, including political representation in the Austrian Reichsrat, education, and bilingualism in the administrative sphere. While the Czechs and other nationalities sought greater national autonomy within the Austrian state, Austrian socialists like Bauer, although promoting a federalist solution, saw themselves as part of the German cultural nation and thus regarded unification with Germany as desirable [176: pp. 214–17]. After the Russian Revolution of 1905, the divisions within the Austrian Socialist Party, particularly between Austrian and Czech delegates, further intensified. These national tensions would result in the split of the multinational Austrian Gesamtpartei into separate national parties. Its formal dissolution occurred in 1911. The trade union movement would meet the same fate before the outbreak of the First World War [Stargardt in 14: pp. 85–6; 176: pp. 195–7].

German socialists and the Polish question

Similar tensions characterised the interaction between German and Polish socialists, particularly after the removal of the anti-socialist laws in 1890 led to a rapprochement between the Social Democrat (SPD) and the German nation-state. Although the outward rhetoric of leading exponents of the SPD still retained its traditional support of the Polish quest for national independence, in their realpolitik they were reluctant to make concessions towards the PPS with regard, for example, to the elections in Silesia, let alone consider the territorial revision in the east of Germany. Some German social democrats were more or less openly in favour of Germanisation (although they often expressed dismay at what they described as Prussia's police methods). Others blatantly asked the Polish socialists to choose between their nationality and their political convictions. In September 1901 – thus roughly a decade before the complete breakdown in relations between Austrian and Czech socialists – the working alliance between the SPD and the Polish Socialist Party in Prussia (PPS) was formally cancelled.

In part, the attitude of the SPD towards the Polish socialists may be attributed to strategic thinking: ten years after the lifting of the anti-socialist laws, the party did not wish to be branded, once again, as *vaterlandslose Gesellen* ('fellows who know no fatherland'). Given the heated atmosphere surrounding the Polish question, such an accusation would have been almost inevitable, as Bismarck's broadsides against

German Catholic conservatives (who were sympathetic to their Polish co-religionists in Prussia) in the 1880s clearly showed. But as Wehler has noted, the SPD's opposition to the national aspirations of the PPS cannot be reduced to a matter of strategy and party discipline in the face of great moral pressure. Rather, around 1900 large sections of the German social democrats had come to the conclusion that German state-nationalism, with its anti-Polish direction, represented a just cause [138: pp. 140–57]. As Wehler commented on this change of attitude to the Polish question in the two decades preceding the First World War: 'It appears that even for the SPD the reality of the consolidated German nation-state had become prevalent to such an extent as to dissipate the former pathos concerning the Polish question' [138: pp. 183–4].

The early Soviet Union: institutionalising nationality at sub-state level

The establishment of the Soviet Union – a vast multinational empire of a new kind – offers an opportunity to examine socialist attitudes to nationality at regime level. Several scholars have shown that the Soviet Union actively supported ethnicity and nationalism. Slezkine has gone so far as to argue that 'Soviet nationality policy was devised and carried out by nationalists' [Slezkine in 172: p. 203]. Yet unlike Germany after 1871 and most of the so-called successor states that were established after the First World War, 'the Soviet Union was never organized, in theory or in practice, as a *Russian* nation-state' [64: p. 28]. There was no attempt, in other words, to create the one and indivisible Soviet nation by imposing Russian culture on the different nationalities living within the boundaries of the Soviet state. Several rulers, including Lenin and Stalin, accepted, and even encouraged, the ethnonational plurality of the state. As Suny writes: 'Soviet Russia was the first state in history to create a federal system based on ethnonational units' [182: p. 141].

If the Soviet leaders of the early hours were nationalists, however, they were so mainly for specific political reasons. As Terry Martin has argued in his path-breaking account of early Soviet nationality policy, the Bolsheviks embraced the slogan of national self-determination because they sought to 'recruit ethnic support for the revolution, not to provide a model for the governing of a multiethnic state' [175: p. 2]. Both Lenin and Stalin were convinced that they would ignore national-ity at their peril, even if they regarded it as a transitory phenomenon that would be overcome through the advancement of socialism. The collapse of the Habsburg and Ottoman empires had exerted a decisive influence on both men. Nations, so they believed, were 'an unavoidable and positive stage in the modernization of the Soviet Union' [175: p. 6]. They also saw the nationality problem in the historical context of oppressed versus oppressor nations, a perspective in which Russia appeared as the guiltiest of all imperialist nationalities. Given its historical legacy of imperialist despotism, Russia, from this point of view, was obliged to make special concessions towards the formerly suppressed nationalities. Both Lenin and Stalin therefore believed it was necessary to grant a certain degree of cultural (not political) autonomy to the various ethnic groups making up the Soviet Union, provided their demands did 'not conflict with a unitary central state' [175: pp. 9–10]. The multinational nature of the Soviet population was recognised in the constitution.

However, there were marked differences among the early leaders of the executive government as to the degree of autonomy that should be granted. Lenin was more tolerant than Stalin, who favoured a more centralist approach. Lenin insisted that all six republics – the Russian Soviet Federated Socialist Republic, Ukraine, Belorussia, Armenia, Azerbaijan and Georgia – should be on an equal footing. As he declared to Kamenev in 1922 in rejection of what he described as Stalin's 'Great Russian Chauvinism': 'I declare war to the death on dominant-nation chauvinism' [cited in 182: p. 142].

But although Stalin, Georgian by ethnicity, would take a more centralist line in all matters concerning politics and administration, he was as federalist as Lenin when it came to culture and language (political and economic national autonomy was opposed by both Lenin and Stalin). Although Russians were the majority and thus dominated government and administration and Russian was 'promoted by the state as its lingua franca' [64: p. 29], there was no programme of Russification that forced the smaller nationalities to adopt Russian culture and language. In fact, what distinguished the 'Soviet system of ethno-territorial federalism' [64: p. 29] from Germany after 1871 and most of the eastern European states of the inter-war period was that it did not pursue large-scale nationalising programmes in the name of national cultural unity. There was no Soviet counterpart to the Magyarisation policies carried out by the Hungarian state between 1867 and 1914.

In the Soviet Union, nationality was institutionalised 'on the sub-state level', but not at the level 'of the state as a whole' [64: p. 29]. The two areas that demonstrate this most clearly are linguistic policy and the issuing of passports. The regime actively encouraged the cultivation and codification of dozens of national languages. A report in the 1920s identified

192 different languages within a still greater number of national territories. Once codified and developed, they would at some point receive official recognition [Slezkine in 172: p. 215; 64: pp. 26–7]. Ethnic nationality – that is, nationality defined in terms of descent – was also institutionalised legally via passports and other personal documents and used for the purpose of administrative surveillance and control. In 1932 this ethnic definition of nationality was introduced as 'an official component of personal status' [64: pp. 30–2].

The 1930s, however, witnessed a fundamental revision of Soviet nationality policy. This revision, which was in significant ways directed against the two largest non-Russian nationalities, the Ukrainians and the Belorussians, reached its apogee during the Great Terror. Ukrainian and Belorussian politicians were branded as 'bourgeois nationalists'. Many were arrested and executed. At the same time, the legitimacy of Russian national culture, identified as it was during the 1920s with great-nation chauvinism, was reinstated. As Terry Martin has written on this Russian nationalist backlash within the Union: 'The Russians and Russian culture were now made the unifying force in a newly imagined Friendship of the Peoples' [175: p. 27]. What determined this shift towards a Russocentric state-nationalism in the 1930s and 1940s was not the revival of socialist universalism, but the totalitarian project of creating the one and indivisible Soviet Union.

Conclusion

The incidents we discussed in Chapter 5 – the split of the Austrian Socialist Party along lines of nationality, the failure of German and Polish socialists to work towards a common goal, or the institutionalisation of ethnicity and nationality in the Soviet Union during the 1920s and 1930s – lend themselves to some concluding reflections on the topic of this book. If nationalism managed to split the socialist movements of Austria and Germany before the outbreak of the First World War, what realistic chance was there that the federalist proposals developed by Bauer and others would be implemented after the war?

The question is difficult to answer. In theory, of course, the implementation of the 'personality principle' proposed by the Austrian socialists would have offered the only chance of preventing the nationality conflict from spiralling out of control. But as Nick Stargardt has noted, it is doubtful whether a federalist multinational state would have worked if it had been established before the outbreak of the war [Stargardt in 14: p. 100]. Even before 1914 nationalism had gathered considerable momentum, not only among the small nationalities within the Austro-Hungarian Empire but also within the large states of central and western Europe. For as Chapter 2 has demonstrated, the German and French authorities embarked on far-reaching projects of cultural, symbolic and political integration designed to strengthen the internal cohesiveness and external competiveness of the nation-state.

After the First World War, the ideological force of nationalism became much enhanced as several new states were created on the principle of national self-determination. As Chapters 3 and 4 have demonstrated, the states that were established after the war or whose territory was enlarged as a result of it were fiercely opposed to granting any cultural and political rights to ethnic and national minorities. Instead, they chose to see it as the right of the majority group to determine the political institutions and the culture within the state. The only government that would institutionalise national cultural autonomy after 1918 – out of a complex blend of ideological and strategic motives – was that of the Soviet Union. It was during the inter-war years, a period marked by political and geopolitical instability, fierce antagonism and status insecurity, that nationalism became an explosive force. It was after 1918 that nationalism, to use Tom Nairn's phrase, became 'a name for the general condition of the modern body politic, more like the climate of political and social thought than just another doctrine' [183: p. 80].

Yet the power of nationalism and national sentiment during the period covered by this book should not be explained by resorting to some kind of psychological reductionism or cultural historicism. Nationalism does not represent some irresistible primordial force or perennial movement. Rather, nationalist movements gathered momentum under conditions that were typical of late nineteenth-century Europe. Rapid industrialisation, increased geographic and social mobility, the extension of democratic rights, state-induced programmes of cultural assimilation, increased inter-state competition, the break-down of institutions and the redrawing of state boundaries, the quest for political and cultural recognition of stateless nationalities – all these factors combined to enhance the role of nationalism in domestic and international politics. In other words, nationalism – its nature, its varying significance, its social and political uses, and its transformation over time – needs to be explained. But once nationalist arguments are widely diffused and institutionalised, as they were in most European states between 1890 and 1940, then they also need to be made part of the explanation. Irrespective, however, of whether we seek to explain nationalism or refer to it in order to explain other phenomena – such as the status and treatment of minority populations, or the rise of fascism – satisfactory answers can only be gained through careful historical contextualisation.

Nor should the fact that, from around 1900 (and certainly during the inter-war period), nationalism began to make conspicuous inroads among the socialist left in central and eastern Europe be taken as proof that nationality will always win out over class solidarities. Europe's history between 1890 and 1940 suggests that allegiance to class and nation should not be seen as mutually exclusive but as linked in powerful ways. Part of nationalism's political force lies precisely in the fact that a significant number of people in Europe had little difficulty in reconciling these two forms of collective identification. Class consciousness, at least in its socially and politically significant manifestations, was rooted in national sentiment. If right-wing nationalism provided an ideological basis for fascist regimes that waged war and committed mass murder, nationalism, albeit of a different kind, also inspired those who fought these regimes at enormous personal cost.

Select Bibliography

This bibliography lists titles thematically in relation to the individual chapters. (The first section on 'Documents and Handbooks' is added to provide additional reference material for those who would like to both deepen and broaden their knowledge in this field.) Those of the works cited which are relevant to more than one chapter have been listed only once. Items that might constitute core readings for courses on the topics covered in the chapters of this book are marked with an asterisk.

Documents and handbooks

[1]   *Omar Dahbour and Micheline R. Ishay (eds), *The Nationalism Reader* (Atlantic Highlands, NJ: Humanities Press, 1995).

[2]   Paula Sutter Fichtner, *The Habsburg Empire: From Dynasticism to Multinationalism* (Malabar, FL: Krieger Publishing Company, 1997).

[3]   Hartmut Lehmann and Silke Lehmann (eds), *Das Nationalitätenproblem in Österreich, 1848–1918* (Göttingen: Vandenhoeck & Ruprecht, 1973).

[4]   *Vincent P. Pecora (ed.), *Nations and Identities: Classic Readings* (Oxford: Blackwell, 2001).

[5]   *John Hutchinson and Anthony D. Smith (eds), *Nationalism* (Oxford University Press, 1994).

[6]   *John Hutchinson and Anthony D. Smith (eds), *Nationalism: Critical Concepts in Political Science* (London: Routledge, 2000).

[7]   Athena Leoussi (ed.), *The Encyclopaedia of Nationalism* (New Brunswick, NJ: Transaction, 2001).

[8]   *Raymond Pearson, *European Nationalism, 1789–1920* (London: Arnold, 1994).

Introduction

[9]   Peter Alter, *Nationalism,* 2nd edn (London: Arnold, 1994).

[10] *Gopal Balakrishnan (ed.), *Mapping the Nation* (London: Verso, 1996).

[11] Marc Bloch, *The Historian's Craft* (Manchester University Press, 1992 [1954]).

[12] Craig Calhoun, *Nationalism* (Buckingham: Open University Press, 1997).

[13] George L. Mosse, 'Racism and Nationalism', *Nations and Nationalism,* 1/2 (1995), pp. 163–73.

[14] Sukumar Periwal (ed.), *Notions of Nationalism* (Budapest: Central European University Press, 1995).

[15] Hagen Schulze, *States, Nations and Nationalism* (Oxford: Blackwell, 1996).

[16] *Anthony D. Smith, *Nationalism and Modernism: A Critical Survey of Recent Theories of Nations and Nationalism* (London: Routledge, 1998).

[17] *Anthony D. Smith, *Nationalism: Theory, Ideology, History* (Cambridge: Polity, 2001).

[18] Mikuláš Teich and Roy Porter (eds), *The National Question in Europe in Historical Context* (Cambridge University Press, 1993).

[19] Stuart Woolf (ed.), *Nationalism in Europe, 1815 to the Present: A Reader* (London/New York: Routledge, 1996).

Chapter 1:   'Nations and Nationalism: Ancient or Modern?'

[20] *Benedict Anderson, *Imagined Communities: Reflections on the Origin and Spread of Nationalism,* new edn (London/New York: Verso, 1991).

[21] Perry Anderson, *Lineages of the Absolutist State* (London/New York: Verso, 1996 [1974]).

[22] Urs Altermatt, *Katholizismus und Moderne. Zur Sozial- und Mentalitätsgeschichte der Schweizer Katholiken im 19. und 20. Jahrhundert* (Zürich: Benziger, 1989).

[23] F. M. Barnard, *J. G. Herder on Social and Political Culture* (Cambridge University Press, 1969).

[24] David A. Bell, *The Cult of the Nation in France: Inventing Nationalism, 1680–1800* (Cambridge, MA: Harvard University Press, 2001).

[25] Isaiah Berlin, *Vico and Herder: Two Studies in the History of Ideas* (London: Hogarth Press, 1976).

[26] Isaiah Berlin, *Against the Current: Essay in the History of Ideas,* ed. Henry Hardy (Oxford: Clarendon, 1979).

[27] T. C. W. Blanning, *The Culture of Power and the Power of Culture: Old Regime Europe, 1660–1789* (Oxford University Press, 2002).

[28] *John Breuilly, *Nationalism and the State,* 2nd edn (Manchester University Press, 1993).

[29] Tony Claydon and Ian McBride (eds), *Protestantism and National Identity: Britain and Ireland, c. 1690–1800* (Cambridge University Press, 1998).

[30] Linda Colley, *Britons: Forging the Nation, 1707–1837* (London: Vintage, 1996).

[31] Karl W. Deutsch and William J. Foltz (eds), *Nation-Building* (New York: Atherton Press, 1966).

[32] Ernest Gellner, *Thought and Change* (London: Weidenfeld and Nicolson, 1964).

[33] *Ernest Gellner, *Nations and Nationalism* (Oxford: Blackwell, 1983).

[34] Ernest Gellner, *Culture, Identity, and Politics* (Cambridge University Press, 1987).

[35] *Ernest Gellner, 'Reply (to Anthony D. Smith): Do Nations Have Navels?', *Nations and Nationalism*, 2/3 (1996), pp. 366–7.

[36] *Philipp Gorski, 'The Mosaic Moment: An Early Modernist Critique of Modernist Theories of Nationalism', *American Journal of Sociology*, 105/5 (March 2000), pp. 1428–68.

[37] *Adrian Hastings, *The Construction of Nationhood: Ethnicity, Religion and Nationalism* (Cambridge University Press, 1997).

[38] *Eric Hobsbawm and Terence Ranger (eds), *The Invention of Tradition* (Cambridge University Press, 1983).

[39] Eric J. Hobsbawm, *The Age of Revolution, 1789–1848* (London: Abacus, 1994 [1962]).

[40] *Eric J. Hobsbawm, *Nations and Nationalism since 1780: Programme, Myth, Reality,* 2nd edn (Cambridge University Press, 1992).

[41] Miroslav Hroch, *Social Preconditions of National Revival in*

Europe: A Comparative Analysis of the Social Composition of Patriotic Groups among the Smaller European Nations (New York: Columbia University Press, 2000 [1985]).

[42] John Hutchinson, *The Dynamics of Cultural Nationalism: The Gaelic Revival and the Creation of the Irish Nation State* (London: Allen & Unwin, 1987).

[43] *Elie Kedourie, *Nationalism*, 4th edn (Oxford: Blackwell, 1993 [1960]).

[44] Dieter Langewiesche, *Nation, Nationalismus und Nationalstaat in Deutschland und Europa* (Munich: C. H. Beck, 2000).

[45] John Plamenatz, 'Two Types of Nationalism', in Eugene Kamenka (ed.), *Nationalism: The Nature and Evolution of an Idea* (London: Edward Arnold, 1976), pp. 23–36.

[46] H. M. Scott (ed.), *Enlightened Absolutism: Reform and Reformers in Later Eighteenth-Century Europe* (Basingstoke: Macmillan – now Palgrave Macmillan, 1990).

[47] Anthony D. Smith, 'Neo-Classicist and Romantic Elements in the Emergence of Nationalist Conceptions', in A. D. Smith (ed.), *Nationalist Movements* (London: Macmillan – now Palgrave Macmillan, 1976).

[48] Anthony D. Smith, *The Ethnic Revival in the Modern World* (Cambridge University Press, 1981).

[49] Anthony D. Smith, *Theories of Nationalism*, 2nd edn (London: Duckworth, 1983).

[50] *Anthony D. Smith, *The Ethnic Origins of Nations* (Oxford: Blackwell, 1986).

[51] *Anthony D. Smith, *National Identity* (Harmondsworth: Penguin, 1991).

[52] Anthony D. Smith, 'Gastronomy or Geology? The Role of Nationalism in the Reconstruction of Nations', *Nations and Nationalism*, 1 (March 1995), pp. 3–24.

[53] Helmut Walser Smith, *German Nationalism and Religious Conflict: Culture, Ideology, Politics, 1870–1914* (Princeton University Press, 1995).

[54] Maurizio Viroli, *For Love of Country: An Essay on Patriotism and Nationalism* (Oxford University Press, 1995).

[55] Oliver Zimmer, *A Contested Nation: History, Memory and Nationalism in Switzerland, 1761–1891* (Cambridge University Press, 2003).

Chapter 2: 'Towards the Mass Nation: Nationalism, Commemoration and Regionalism'

[56]   Wolfgang Altgeld, 'Religion, Denomination and Nationalism in Nineteenth-Century Germany', in Helmut Walser Smith (ed.), *Protestants, Catholics and Jews in Germany, 1800–1914* (Oxford: Berg, 2001), pp. 49–66.

[57]   *Celia Applegate, *A Nation of Provincials: The German Idea of Heimat* (Berkeley: University of California Press, 1990).

[58]   Celia Applegate, 'A Europe of Regions: Reflections on the Historiography of Sub-National Places in Modern Times', *American Historical Review*, 104 (Oct 1999), pp. 1157–182.

[59]   Jay W. Baird, *To Die for Germany: Heroes in the Nazi Pantheon* (Bloomington: Indiana University Press, 1990), pp. 41–72.

[60]   Stefan Berger, Mark Donovan and Kevin Passmore (eds), *Writing National Histories: Western Europe since 1800* (London/New York: Routledge, 1999).

[61]   Volker Berghahn, *Imperial Germany, 1871–1914: Economy, Society, Culture and Politics* (Oxford/Providence, RI: Berghahn Books, 1994).

[62]   *John Breuilly, 'Nationalism and the History of Ideas', *Proceedings of the British Academy*, 105 (2000), pp. 187–223.

[63]   John Breuilly (ed.), *19th-century Germany: Politics, Culture and Society, 1780–1918* (London: Arnold, 2001).

[64]   *Rogers Brubaker, *Nationalism Reframed: Nationhood and the National Question in the New Europe* (Cambridge University Press, 1996).

[65]   *Alon Confino, *The Nation as a Local Metaphor: Württemberg, Imperial Germany, and National Memory, 1871–1918* (Chapel Hill, NC/London: University of North Carolina Press, 1997).

[66]   Walker Connor, *Ethnonationalism: The Quest for Understanding* (Princeton University Press, 1994).

[67]   Dieter Düding et al. (eds), *Öffentliche Festkultur: Politische Feste in Deutschland von der Aufklärung bis zum Ersten Weltkrieg* (Hamburg: Rowohlt, 1988).

[68]   *Caroline Ford, *Creating the Nation in Provincial France: Religion and Political Identity in Brittany* (Princeton University Press, 1993).

[69]   Alain Forrest, 'Federalism', in Colin Lucas (ed.), *The French Revolution and the Creation of Modern Political Culture*, 2 vols. (Oxford University Press, 1988), vol. 2, pp. 309–27.

128

[70] Etienne François et al. (eds), *Nation und Emotion: Deutschland und Frankreich im Vergleich im 19. und 20. Jahrhundert* (Göttingen: Vandenhoeck & Ruprecht, 1995).

[71] *Anthony Giddens, *The Nation-State and Violence*, vol. 2 of *A Contemporary Critique of Historical Materialism* (Cambridge: Polity, 1985), chs. 4 and 8.

[72] Robert Gildea, *Barricades and Borders: Europe, 1800–1914*, 2nd edn (Oxford University Press, 1996).

[73] *John R. Gillis (ed.), *Commemorations: The Politics of National Identity* (Princeton University Press, 1994).

[74] Raoul Girardet (ed.), *Le Nationalism français, 1871–1914* (Paris: A. Colin, 1966).

[75] Svenja Goltermann, *Körper der Nation: Habitusformierung und die Politik des Turnens, 1860–1890* (Göttingen: Vandenhoeck & Ruprecht, 1998).

[76] Wolfgang Hardtwig, 'Geschichtsinteresse, Geschichtsbilder und politische Symbole in der Reichsgründungsära und im Kaiserreich', in E. Mai and S. Waetzoldt (eds), *Kunstverwaltung, Bau- und Denkmal-Politik im Kaiserreich* (Berlin: Gebrüder Mann Verlag, 1981).

[77] Pierre-Jakez Héliaz, *The Horse of Pride: Life in a Breton Village* (London/New Haven, CN: Yale University Press, 1978).

[78] *Eric J. Hobsbawm, *The Age of Empire, 1875–1914* (London: Abacus, 1987).

[79] Michael Jeismann, *Das Vaterland der Feinde: Studien zum nationalen Feindbegriff und Selbstverständnis in Deutschland und Frankreich, 1792–1918* (Stuttgart: Klett-Cotta, 1992).

[80] D. Langewiesche and G. Schmidt (eds), *Föderative Nation* (Berlin: Oldenbourg, 2001).

[81] * James R. Lehning, *Peasants and French: Cultural Contact in Rural France during the Nineteenth Century* (Cambridge University Press, 1995).

[82] Michael Mann, *The Sources of Social Power, vol. II: The Rise of Classes and Nation-states, 1760–1914* (Cambridge University Press, 1993), chs. 3, 7, 20.

[83] Patricia Mazón, 'Germania Triumphant: The Niederwald National Monument and the Liberal Moment in Imperial Germany', *German History*, 8/2 (2000), pp. 162–92.

[84] Wolfgang J. Mommsen, *Max Weber and German Politics, 1890–1920* (Chicago University Press, 1984).

[85] Wolfgang J. Mommsen, 'The Varieties of the Nation State in Modern History: Liberal, Imperialist, Fascist and Contemporary Notions of Nation and Nationality', in M. Mann (ed.), *The Rise and Decline of the Nation State* (Oxford, 1990), pp. 210–26.

[86] *George L. Mosse, *Fallen Soldiers: Reshaping the Memory of the World Wars* (Oxford University Press, 1990).

[87] *George L. Mosse, *The Nationalization of the Masses: Political Symbolism and Mass Movements in Germany from the Napoleonic Wars through the Third Reich,* new edn (Ithaca, NY: Cornell University Press, 1991).

[88] Thomas Nipperdey, *Deutsche Geschichte, 1866–1918*, vols. 1 and 2 (Munich: C. H. Beck, 1998).

[89] **Realms of Memory: The Construction of the French Past*, under the direction of Pierre Nora, 3 vols. (New York: Columbia University Press, 1996–8).

[90] James Retallack, *Germany in the Age of Kaiser Wilhelm II* (Basingstoke: Macmillan – now Palgrave Macmillan, 1996).

[91] James Retallack (ed.), *Saxony in German History: Culture, Society, and Politics, 1830–1933* (Ann Arbor: University of Michigan Press, 2000).

[92] Daniel J. Sherman, 'Art, Commerce, and the Production of Memory in France after World War I', in John R. Gillis (ed.), *Commemorations: The Politics of National Identity* (Princeton University Press, 1994), pp. 186–211.

[93] Charles Tilly (ed.), *The Formation of National States in Western Europe* (Princeton University Press, 1975).

[94] Robert Tombs, *France, 1814–1914* (London: Longman, 1996).

[95] Maiken Umbach (ed.), *German Federalism* (Basingstoke: Palgrave Macmillan, 2002).

[96] Jakob Vogel, *Nationen im Gleichschritt: Der Kult der 'Nation in Waffen' in Deutschland und Frankreich, 1871–1914* (Göttingen: Vandenhoeck & Ruprecht, 1995).

[97] *Eugen Weber, *Peasants into Frenchmen: The Modernisation of Rural France* (Stanford University Press, 1976).

[98] Eugen Weber, *My France: Politics, Culture, Myth* (Cambridge, MA: Belknap Press, 1991).

[99] Eugen Weber, 'What Rough Beast?', *Critical Review*, 10/2 (Spring 1996), pp. 285–98.

[100] Hans-Ulrich Wehler, *Deutsche Gesellschaftsgeschichte,* vol. 3 (Munich: C. H. Beck, 1995).

[101] Michael Winock, *Nationalism, Anti-Semitism and Fascism in France* (Stanford University Press, 1998).

[102] Oliver Zimmer, 'Competing Memories of the Nation: Liberal Historians and the Reconstruction of the Swiss Past', *Past and Present*, 168 (2000), pp. 194–226.

Chapter 3: 'Boundaries of National Belonging: Nationalism and the Minorities Question'

[103] Martin Broszat, *Zweihundert Jahre deutsche Polenpolitik* (Frankfurt: Suhrkamp, 1990).

[104] *Maria Bucur and Nancy M. Wingfield (eds), *Staging the Past: The Politics of Commemoration in Habsburg Central Europe: 1848 to the Present* (West Lafayette: Indiana University Press, 2001).

[105] Neil Caplan, 'Review Article: Talking Zionism, Doing Zionism, Studying Zionism', *Historical Journal*, 44/4 (2001), pp. 1083–97.

[106] Norman Davies, *God's Playground: A History of Poland, vol. 2: 1795 to the Present* (Oxford University Press, 1981).

[107] István Deák, 'The Habsburg Empire', in Karen Barkey and Mark von Hagen (eds), *After Empire: Multiethnic Societies and Nation-Building: The Soviet Union and the Russian, Ottoman, and Habsburg Empires* (Colorado/Oxford: Westview Press, 1997), pp. 129–41.

[108] Geoff Eley, 'German Politics and Polish Nationality: The Dialectic of Nation-Forming in the East of Prussia', *East European Quarterly*, 18/3 (Sept 1984), pp. 335–64.

[109] *Paula Sutter Fichtner, *The Habsburg Empire: From Dynasticism to Multinationalism* (Malabar, FL: Krieger Publishing Company, 1997).

[110] *Carole Fink, 'Defender of Minorities: Germany in the League of Nations, 1926–1933', *Central European History*, 4 (1972), pp. 330–57.

[111] Michael Forman, *Nationalism and the International Labor Movement: The Idea of the Nation in Socialist and Anarchist Theory* (Penn State University Press, 1998).

[112] Dieter Gosewinkel, *Einbürgern und Ausschliessen: Die Nationalisierung der Staatsangehörigkeit vom Deutschen Bund*

bis zur Bundesrepublik Deutschland (Göttingen: Vandenhoeck & Ruprecht, 2001).

[113] William W. Hagen, 'Murder in the East: German–Jewish Liberal Reactions to Anti-Jewish Violence in Poland and Other East European Lands, 1918–1920', *Central European History*, 34/1 (2001), pp. 1–30.

[114] Michael Hechter, *Containing Nationalism* (Oxford University Press, 2000).

[115] Patrice Higonnet, *Goodness Beyond Virtue* (Cambridge, MA: Harvard University Press, 1998).

[116] *Michael John, '"We Do Not Even Possess Our Selves": On Identity and Ethnicity in Austria, 1880–1937', *Austrian History Yearbook*, 30 (1999), pp. 17–64.

[117] Eugen Kalkschmidt (ed.), *Bismarcks Reden* (Berlin, n.d.).

[118] *Dominic Lieven, 'Dilemmas of Empire, 1850–1918: Power, Territory, Identity', *Journal of Contemporary History*, 34/2 (1999), pp. 163–200.

[119] *Irina Livezeanu, *Cultural Politics in Greater Romania: Regionalism, Nation Building, & Ethnic Struggle, 1918–1930* (Ithaca, NY: Cornell University Press, 1995).

[120] C. A. Macartney, *Hungary: A Short History* (Edinburgh University Press, 1961).

[121] Mark Mazower, *Dark Continent: Europe's Twentieth Century* (Harmondsworth: Penguin, 1998), ch. 2.

[122] *Ezra Mendelsohn, *The Jews of East Central Europe between the World Wars* (Bloomington: Indiana University Press, 1983).

[123] Ezra Mendelsohn (ed.), *Essential Papers on Jews and the Left* (New York: NYU Press, 1997).

[124] Wolfgang J. Mommsen, 'Nationalität im Zeichen offensiver Weltpolitik: Das Reichs- und Staatsangehörigkeitsgesetz des Deutschen Reiches vom 22. Juni 1913', in M. Hettling and P. Nolte (eds), *Nation und Gesellschaft in Deutschland: Historische Essays* (Munich: C. H. Beck, 1996), pp. 128–41.

[125] Hans J. Morgenthau, *Politics Among Nations: The Struggle for Power and Peace,* 5th edn (New York: Alfred A. Knopf, 1978).

[126] Robin Okey, *Eastern Europe, 1740–1985: Feudalism to Communism*, 2nd edn (London/New York: Routledge, 1992).

[127] Mona Ozouf, *Festivals and the French Revolution* (Cambridge, MA: Harvard University Press, 1988).

[128] *Raymond Pearson, *National Minorities in Eastern Europe,*

1848–1945 (Basingstoke: Macmillan – now Palgrave Macmillan, 1983).

[129] *Joseph Rothschild, *East Central Europe between the Two World Wars* (Seattle and London: University of Washington Press, 1974).

[130] R. W. Seton-Watson, *Masaryk in England* (Cambridge University Press, 1943).

[131] *Alan Sked, *The Decline and Fall of the Habsburg Empire, 1815–1918* (London: Pearson, 2001 [1989]).

[132] Anthony D. Smith, 'Chosen Peoples: Why Ethnic Groups Survive', *Ethnic and Racial Studies*, 15/3 (July 1992), pp. 436–56.

[133] Michael Stanislawski, *Zionism and the Fin de Siècle: Cosmopolitanism and Nationalism from Nordau to Jabotinski* (Berkeley: University of California Press, 2001).

[134] *David Vital, *Zionism: The Crucial Phase* (Oxford University Press, 1987).

[135] Andrzej Walicki, *Philosophy and Romantic Nationalism: The Case of Poland* (University of Notre Dame Press, 1994).

[136] Piotr Wandycz, *The Price of Freedom: A History of East Central Europe from the Middle Ages to the Present* (London: Harper Collins, 1992).

[137] *Solomon Wank, 'Some Reflections on the Habsburg Empire and Its Legacy in the Nationalities Question', *Austrian History Yearbook*, 28 (1997), pp. 131–46.

[138] Hans-Ulrich Wehler, *Sozialdemokratie und Nationalstaat* (Göttingen: Vandenhoeck & Ruprecht, 1971).

[139] *Nancy M. Wingfield, 'Conflicting Constructions of Memory: Attacks on Statues of Joseph II in the Bohemian Lands after the Great War', *Austrian History Yearbook*, 28 (1997), pp. 147–71.

Chapter 4:   'Homeland Nationalism Gone Wild: Nationalism and Fascism'

[140] *Martin Blinkhorn (ed.), *Fascists and Conservatives: The Radical Right and the Establishment of Twentieth-century Europe* (London: Unwin Hyman, 1990).

[141] *Rogers Brubaker, *Citizenship and Nationhood in France and Germany* (Cambridge, MA: Harvard University Press, 1992).

[142] Geoff Eley, *From Unification to Nazism: Reinterpreting the German Past* (Boston and London: Allen & Unwin, 1986).

[143] *Andreas K. Fahrmeir, 'Nineteenth-Century German Citizenships: A Reconsideration', *Historical Journal*, 40/3 (1997), pp. 721–52.

[144] Stephen Fischer-Galati, 'Fascism in Romania', in Peter F. Sugar (ed.), *Native Fascism in the Successor States, 1918–1945* (Santa Barbara: ABC-Clio, 1971), pp. 112–21.

[145] Peter Gilg and Erich Gruner, 'Nationale Erneuerungsbewegungen in der Schweiz, 1925–1940', *Vierteljahreshefte für Zeitgeschichte*, 14 (1966), pp. 1–25.

[146] Beat Glaus, *Die Nationale Front: Eine Schweizer Faschistische Bewegung, 1930–1940* (Zürich: Benziger, 1969).

[147] *Roger Griffin, *The Nature of Fascism* (London/New York: Routledge, 1991).

[148] *Roger Griffin (ed.), *International Fascism: Theories, Causes and the New Consensus* (London: Arnold, 1998).

[149] Roger Griffin, 'The Primacy of Culture: The Current Growth (or Manufacture) of Consensus within Fascist Studies', *Journal of Contemporary History*, 37/3 (2002), pp. 21–43.

[150] Eric J. Hobsbawm, *Age of Extremes: The Short Twentieth Century, 1914–1991* (London: Abacus, 1994).

[151] Martyn Housden, 'Ewald Ammende and the Organization of National Minorities in Inter-war Europe', *German History*, 18/4 (2000), pp. 439–60.

[152] Martin Kitchen, *Europe between the Wars: A Political History* (London: Longman, 1988).

[153] *Walter Lacquer (ed.), *Fascism: A Reader's Guide* (New York: Howard Fertig, 1976).

[154] *Stein Ugelvik Larsen, Bernt Hagtvet and Jan Petter Myklebust (eds), *Who were the Fascists? Social Roots of European Fascism* (Bergen/Oslo: Universitetsforlaget, 1980).

[155] Vladimir Ilyich Lenin, 'The Right of Nations to Self-Determination', in Omar Dahbour and Micheline R. Ishay (eds), *The Nationalism Reader* (New Jersey: Humanities Press, 1995 [1907]), pp. 208–14.

[156] Juan J. Linz, 'Some Notes Toward a Comparative Study of Fascism in Sociological Historical Perspective', in Walter Lacquer (ed.), *Fascism: A Reader's Guide* (New York: Howard Fertig, 1976), pp. 3–124.

[157] *George L. Mosse, *Confronting the Nation: Jewish and Western*

Nationalism (Hanover/London: University Press of New England, 1993).

[158] *George L. Mosse, *The Fascist Revolution: Toward a General Theory of Fascism* (New York: Howard Fertig, 1999).

[159] J. Noakes and G. Pridham (eds), *Nazism, 1919–1945: A Documentary Reader*, vol. 1 (University of Exeter Press, 1983).

[160] *Robert O. Paxton, 'Five Stages of Fascism', *Journal of Modern History*, 70 (1998), pp. 1–23.

[161] *Stanley Payne, *A History of Fascism, 1914–1945* (London: UCL Press, 1995).

[162] Oswald Sigg, *Die eidgenössischen Volksinitiativen, 1892–1939* (Bern: Haupt, 1978).

[163] *Anthony D. Smith, *Nationalism in the Twentieth Century* (Oxford: Martin Robertson, 1979), ch. 3.

[164] *Zeev Sternhell, *The Birth of Fascist Ideology* (Princeton University Press, 1994).

[165] Peter F. Sugar (ed.), *A History of Hungary* (Bloomington: Indiana University Press, 1990).

[166] *Peter F. Sugar (ed.), *Eastern European Nationalism in the 20th Century* (Washington: American University Press, 1995).

[167] Emanuel Turczynski, 'The Background of Romanian Fascism', in Peter F. Sugar (ed.), *Native Fascism in the Successor States, 1918–1945* (Santa Barbara: ABC-Clio, 1971), pp. 101–11.

[168] Oliver Zimmer, 'Die "Volksgemeinschaft": Entstehung und Funktion einer nationalen Einheitssemantik in der Krise der 30er Jahre in der Schweiz', in K. Imhof, H. Kleger and G. Romano (eds), *Krise und sozialer Wandel, vol. II: Konkordanz und Kalter Krieg* (Zürich: Seismo, 1996), pp. 85–110.

[169] Oliver Zimmer, '"A unique fusion of the natural and the man-made": The Trajectory of Swiss Nationalism, 1933–1939', *Journal of Contemporary History*, forthcoming.

Chapter 5:   'Nationalism and its Critics'

[170] Maurice Agulhon, *The Republican Experiment, 1848–1852* (Cambridge University Press, 1983).

[171] John Breuilly, *The Formation of the First German Nation-State, 1800–1871* (Basingstoke: Macmillan – now Palgrave Macmillan, 1996).

[172] Geoff Eley and Ronald G. Suny (eds), *Becoming National: A Reader* (Oxford University Press, 1996).

[173] Abigail Green, *Fatherlands: State-Building and Nationhood in Nineteenth-Century Germany* (Cambridge University Press, 2001).

[174] Georges Haupt, Michaël Löwy and Claudie Weill (eds), *Les Marxistes et La Question Nationale, 1848–1914*, 2nd edn (Paris: Éditions L'Harmattan, 1997).

[175] *Terry Martin, *The Affirmative Action Empire: Nations and Nationalism in the Soviet Union, 1923–1939* (Ithaca, NY: Cornell University Press, 2001).

[176] Hans Mommsen, *Arbeiterbewegung und Nationale Frage* (Göttingen: Vandenhoeck & Ruprecht, 1979).

[177] *Ephraim Nimni, *Marxism and Nationalism: Theoretical Origins of a Political Crisis* (London: Pluto Press, 1991).

[178] Thomas Nipperdey, *Deutsche Geschichte, 1800–1866: Bürgerwelt und starker Staat* (Munich: C. H. Beck, 1998).

[179] Edward Shils, 'Nation, Nationality, Nationalism and Civil Society', *Nations and Nationalism*, 1/1 (March 1995), pp. 93–118.

[180] Wolfram Siemann, *The German Revolution of 1848–49* (Basingstoke: Macmillan – now Palgrave Macmillan, 1998).

[181] Jonathan Sperber, *The European Revolutions, 1848–1851* (Cambridge University Press, 1994).

[182] *Ronald Grigor Suny, *The Soviet Experiment: Russia, the USSR, and the Successor States* (Oxford University Press, 1998).

Conclusion

[183] Tom Nairn, *Faces of Nationalism: Janus Revisited* (London/New York: Verso, 1997).

Appendix

Table 1: Populations (in millions) of European states and nations, 1850–1920

	1850	1900	1920
Austria	17.5	26.2	6.5
Belgium	4.4	6.7	7.4
Bulgaria	–	3.5	4.8
Czechoslovakia	–	–	13.6
Denmark	1.4	2.5	3.1
Finland	1.6	2.7	3.2
France	35.7	38.9	39.2
Germany	35.2	56.4	61.0
Greece	1.0	2.5	5.0
Habsburg Empire	30.7	45.5	–
Hungary	13.2	19.3	8.0
Ireland	6.6	4.5	2.8
Italy	24.4	33.0	38.0
Ottoman Empire in Europe	16.0	5.7	–
Poland	–	15.1	27.2
Prussia	16.4	33.5	–
Rumania	3.9	6.0	15.0
Russian Empire	68.5	130.0	145.0
Scotland	2.8	4.4	4.8
Serbia	–	2.4	–
Spain	14.0	18.6	21.0
Sweden	3.5	5.1	5.8
Switzerland	2.4	3.3	3.9
United Kingdom	27.2	41.0	42.0
Yugoslavia	–	–	12.0

Source: Raymond Pearson, *European Nationalism, 1789–1920* (London: Longman, 1994), p. 237.

Table 2: National minorities in the east European states, 1919–38

State	Census year	Minorities as % of total population	
		By census	*By estimate*
Albania	1930	22.3	24
Bulgaria	1934	13.3	16
Czechoslovakia	1921	undifferentiated	52
Estonia	1934	11.8	13
Hungary	1920	10.4	15
Latvia	1930	26.6	28
Lithuania	1923	16.1	18
Poland	1921	30.8	35
Romania	1930	29.2	34
Yugoslavia	1931	undifferentiated	57
Average		20.1	29.2

Note: Official censuses tended to underplay the representation of minorities. The table thus contains statistics from both the appropriate state census and estimates by reputable contemporary authorities.
Source: Raymond Pearson, *National Minorities in Eastern Europe, 1848–1945* (London: Macmillan – now Palgrave Macmillan, 1983), p. 148.

Table 3: Ethnic composition of Austria–Hungary (in millions) in 1910

Nationality	Population	% of total
Germans	12.0	23.9
Magyars	10.0	20.2
Czechs	6.5	12.6
Poles	5.0	10.0
Ruthenians	4.0	7.9
Romanians	3.25	6.4
Croats	2.5	5.3
Slovaks	2.0	3.8
Serbs	2.0	3.8
Slovenes	1.25	2.6
Others (incl. Italians)	2.9	3.5
Total	51.4	100.0

Source: Raymond Pearson, *European Nationalism, 1789–1920* (London: Longman, 1994), p. 239.

Table 4: Religious affiliation in Austria–Hungary (in millions) in 1910

Religion	Population	% of total
Roman Catholic (incl. Uniate)	39.0	77.2
Protestant	4.5	8.9
Orthodox	4.5	8.9
Jewish	2.1	3.9
Muslim	0.5	1.1
Total	50.6	100.0

Source: Raymond Pearson, *European Nationalism, 1789–1920* (London: Longman, 1994), p. 240.

Table 5: National composition of Poland (census of 1921)

Nationality	Population	% of total
Poles	18 814 000	69.2
Ruthenes	3 898 000	14.3
Jews	2 110 000	7.8
Belorussians	1 060 000	3.9
Germans	1 059 000	3.9
Lithuanians	69 000	0.3
Russians	56 000	0.2
Czechs	31 000	0.1
Others	78 000	0.3
Total	27 177 000	100.0

Source: Raymond Pearson, *National Minorities in Eastern Europe, 1848–1945* (London: Macmillan – now Palgrave Macmillan, 1983), p. 163.

Table 6: National composition of Romania (census of 1930)

Nationality	Population	% of total
Romanians	12 981 000	70.8
Magyars	1 426 000	8.6
Germans	745 000	4.2
Jews	728 000	4.1
Russians	409 000	2.3
Ruthenes/Ukrainians	382 000	2.2
Bulgars	366 000	2.1
Gypsies	263 000	1.5
Turks	177 000	0.9
Others	418 000	2.4
Total	17 895 000	100.0

Source: Raymond Pearson, *National Minorities in Eastern Europe, 1848–1945* (London: Macmillan – now Palgrave Macmillan, 1983), p. 163.

Table 7: National composition of Czechoslovakia (census of 1930)

Nationality	Population	% of total
Czecho-Slovaks	9 750 000	64.1
Germans	3 318 000	22.5
Magyars	720 000	4.9
Ruthenes	569 000	3.9
Jews	205 000	1.4
Poles	100 000	0.7
Gypsies	33 000	0.2
Others	35 000	0.2
Total	14 730 000	98.9

Source: Raymond Pearson, *National Minorities in Eastern Europe, 1848–1945* (London: Macmillan – now Palgrave Macmillan, 1983), p. 152.

Table 8:   Trianon losses and residues (per 1910 data)

	Area (sq. km)	Population (total)	Magyars (linguistic)
Historic Hungary (without Croatia–Slavonia)	282 870	18 264 533	9 944 627
Lost to:			
Austria	4 020	291 618	26 153
Czechoslovakia	61 633	3 517 568	1 066 685
Poland	589	23 662	230
Romania	103 093	5 257 467	1 661 805
Yugoslavia	20 551	1 509 295	452 265
Italy	21	49 806	6 493
Total losses	189 907	10 649 416	3 213 631
Residual Hungary	92 963	7 615 117	6 730 996

Source: Joseph Rothschild, *East Central Europe between the Two World Wars* (University of Washington Press, 1974), p. 155.

Index

and pre-modern church, 21
and class solidarity, 122–3
conservative thinkers and, 108
critics of modernist explanations of,
  15–18
as cultural construction, 13–15
definition of, 17–18
and Enlightened absolutism, 8
and 'ethnosymbolism', 20–1
and historicism, 8–9
as ideology, 5–7
as 'imagined political community', 14
and imperialism, 36–8
and industrialism, 11–13
and inter-state competition, 35–6
and 'invented traditions', 13–14
and irredentism, 61
liberal attitudes to, 109–10
as a mass phenomenon, 27–8
and memories of former statehood,
  25
and the modernist consensus, 4–18
and modern mass democracy, 13, 28,
  33–4
and modern mass sports, 38
and (pre-modern) national
  consciousness, 18
and national self-determination, 60
and the nationalising state, 27–9
and patriotism, 25
as a political movement, 9–11
and 'print-capitalism', 14
and 'proto-nationalism', 19
and regionalism, 45–9
and religion, 24–5
teleological fallacy, 2
see also fascism; minority populations;
  successor states
Nazi Germany, 1
  Lebensraum, 104
  support for Lebensraum ideology
    among borderland populations,
    105
  Weimar homeland nationalism, 104
  see also fascism; nationalism; German
    Empire; Weimar Germany
Netherlands, 1, 24
Nietzsche, Friedrich, 85
Nipperdey, Thomas, 38, 112
Norwegians, 26

Palacky, Frantisek, 57
Pan-German League, 55
Paxton, Robert O., 83, 86
Payne, Stanley, 82–3, 93

peace settlements, 1, 60–1
  see also minority populations;
    successor states
Pittsburgh Agreement (1918), 70
Poland (state)
  Belorussians, 63
  Germans, 63
  Jews, 63
  Lithuanians, 63
  minorities, 63–4
  political parties, 63–4
  'school strike' in Upper Silesia (1926),
    64–5
  Ukrainians, 63–4
  see also peace settlements; successor
    states
Poles, 3, 24, 25, 26
  division of Poland–Lithuania, 53
  May Laws of 1873, 54–5
  Poles in Prussia, 53
  Polish uprisings, 54
  repression by Prussian state, 54–5
  see also German Empire; Poland
Prost, Antoine, 43
public commemorations, festivals and
    monuments, 39
  Bismarck monuments, 42
  Eiffel Tower, 36
  Exhibition Universelle, 36
  fallen soldiers (First World War), 43–4,
    47–9
  Kaiserparaden, 39
  role of popular mass associations, 41
  Sedan Day celebrations, 40, 46
  Swiss National Museum, 35
  see also nationalism

Renan, Ernest, 1
Renner, Karl, 112, 115
Romania, 3
  anti-Semitism, 95
  Bukovina, 67
  demographic structure, 65–6
  educational cultural initiative, 66–8
  emancipation of Jews and its reversal, 96
  and fascism, 90
  Greater Romania, 65, 95
  and Hungarian revisionism, 95
  independence of 1878, 65
  Iron Guard, 97
  League of National Christian Defence, 97
  official policy towards minorities, 66–9,
    95
  territorial acquisitions after the First
    World War, 66

145